The Run of Myself

Poems, Songs, and Stories
Joseph McConnell

PA
ProcArch
Press

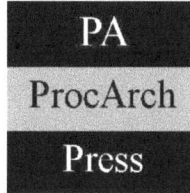

ProcArch LLC, Ann Arbor

Cover design by the author. Photos by the author, copyright (front) 2017, (back) 1981.

ISBN: 978-0-9963385-4-7

Second edition, 2017.

This book is for Linda and Patrick and Charlotte and Orion and Felix.

Contents

Introduction i

Poems 1

    Wearing Cleats 1

    The East 2

    A Used Textbook 3

    The Muddy Dog 4

    Sailing to Vladivostok 5

    The Nightmare 7

    A Line of Lorca's 8

    The Harper 9

    A Dog Doesn't Wonder 9

    Black Pool 10

    An Agincourt Trefoil 11

        Agincourt One 11

        Agincourt Two 12

        Agincourt Three 13

    An Individual Obsession 16

    Sessions 18

    Passing By 19

    In the Hospital 20

    Federico Garcia Lorca 21

    Temptation and Revision 23

    After the Funeral 25

    Growing Uncaring 26

    Marriage Equality Referendum, Ireland 28

    UPS 29

    Leader Dog Blues 30

Neither drink nor feasting 31

Replacing a tree.. 33

The Stone Boat.. 34

Hide and Go Find 35

One Evening 36

Business Cards.. 38

The Old Man Himself 39

Songs 41

A Holiday Anthem 41

Marches, camps, and Empire... 42

Proceedings Set to Waltz Time 43

Stories 45

Antiquities 45

Of Marginal Interest 56

The Assault on Cerro Roja 60

The Featureless Plain 61

Waren Trust 65

The Remnant... 69

The Bodies 83

The Station at Avignon.. 92

The Author 96

__Introduction__

Neither here nor in most of my other writing will you find much explanation. For me, the pleasure of doing this comes in the moment when I realize that I can just stop, just leave it up to you to answer your questions.

"Why did your character do that?"

"Why do you think she did it?"

If this sounds familiar, it should. It's not a new approach to fiction, poetry, or any other kind of expression. A symbol is a symbol, and it isn't and can't be the thing it symbolizes, whether it's framed as a story, a picture, or as a Venus figurine. Some symbols go farther down the road; they spend more time fleshing out the details, but they're still symbols, and they still require you to translate them into your personal version of the original. I just enjoy seeing how little language I can use and still, I hope, give your mind and experience something to work on.

As far as poetry goes, I'm with Archibald MacLeish when he says, in *Ars Poetica*, "A poem should not mean but be." I'm fairly confident that most of mine are. Beyond that, they're either deliberately symbolic or they aren't. Some are just word play.

The prose bits here are products, some of them, of actual dreams, or the kind of waking dream you experience when you're awake but would really rather be asleep. And the little play would have been a short story, but I wanted to experiment with writing in a theatre form. And it still had its basis in a dream.

Anyway, however you react to any of this, unless you simply read one word at a time without thinking about it, your response is your own fault. Don't blame me.

Poems

These verses were written between 1982 and 2017, and they vary as much as you might expect over those 35 years.

Wearing Cleats   *2015*

Stand on the street.
Be inconspicuous.
Watch us go by,
The older guys.
One in three has given up.
But you wait for the one
Who hasn't yet
Lost the run of himself,
Who sees the snake
And still dodges the strike,
Who'll take your hand
For balance,
Cracking wise,
And walk the icy sidewalk with you
Into another winter.

The East

The sunrise
In the east was red.
The sails of the regatta
Are coming down
Against coming heavy weather.
Short of expectation,
They're fluttering and falling like leaves,
Backlit red as leaves in the fall.
Why is this one boat
Any sadder than the others?
It was mine.

A Used Textbook

Thirty years ago
My mother recommended to me
An old anthology
Of poetry: A.J.M. Smith's
Seven Centuries of Verse.

I bought a used copy,
And it was full
Of the worst struggling notes
In someone's hand
Trying to understand
Yeats and Hopkins
On a public school education.

"Poet is split into two
This separates him from animal part"
Whatever this meant
To some poor sod

Copying down blindly the phrase
Of a bored TA in Humanities
Nothing does it impart
Of the first two lines
Of *Sailing to Byzantium.*

And apparently
There was nothing to be said
(No notes appear)
Of *Byzantium*'s first two lines
That end, "The Emperor's drunken soldiery are abed".

3

The Muddy Dog

2013

Between the church and the synagogue
There was a man, mired in a bog.
He tried to touch the face of God,
But his face was licked by a muddy dog.

As time went on, he wondered why
He got no answers from the sky.
His spirit faltered and began to fail,
But he pulled himself out by the muddy dog's tail.

He and the dog walked slowly home
And left religion on its own.
He planted crops and drained the bog,
And lived out his life with the muddy dog.

Sailing to Vladivostok

Panic was easy enough to come by
Down by the Dogger Bank,
When the sea was full of dancing lights
And dim shapes that might have been God knows what
Torpedo boats or anything at all.
And they opened fire, the Czar's fleet,
On British fishermen,
There in the fog.

Steel hulls, men, boxes of machinery
Steaming from the Baltic,
Sent around the world
To reinforce failure:
The embodiment of Imperial Russia.
They weren't new ships,
Or even ships of uniform design,
The Russians didn't build in classes often,
But in ones and twos, haphazardly,
With the funds that trickled through
Layers of corrupt administration.

How to say it? The fleet was a *thing*.
It was an act,
Something actually done,
Different from the daily getting by
And carrying on
That a bureaucracy performs.

And when doing is the exception

And getting by is the rule,
The things that do get done
Reflect those who do them.
And that may be all they're good for,
And their only value.

And so Russia sent an image of itself
Through the English Channel,
Past Gibraltar, around the Cape for Asia.
Tied to the speed of its slowest ship,
Led by Rozhestvenski to their deaths.

And the sailors must have talked and thought
Hearing the engines thumping all night long,
Looking out the casemates day by day
Along the barrels of their guns
Stoking the fires
Stowing the hammocks in the messes
Serving meals.
They must have speculated,
Must have convinced themselves.
That there would be at least some self-respect.

The Nightmare 2012

Did you ever have a nightmare
Where you'd foreseen it all?
Where you'd seen the helldoor open,
And the sky fall?

Run through the smoking forest
Wearing concrete shoes.
Seen the bullet coming,
Nothing you could do?

We saw the nightmare starting
Twenty years ago.
We rode a Persian carpet
Flying far too low.

We saw the water rising,
And we smelled the smoky wind.
I'm sure I tried to warn you ...
Can't remember when.

A Line of Lorca's

2003

"The dark archers approach Seville"
Federico Garcia Lorca, Poem of the Saeta

The patient digger scraping humus
From an object he misunderstands
Calls it a fetish; the chorus intones:
Fetishes, idols, mother gods, bones.

    Is it mystic to belong to your past?
    Was Lorca a mystic for knowing
    The sandy wind from Africa blowing
    What Spain had been?

Pinch in soft clay a rude portrait of your aunt;
Hear us call it Venus.

    The mystic music in the incense shop,
    Was born of a deer skin
    Stretched across an alder hoop,
    Thumped by a heart-sick, half-bright boy
    While his betters danced.

Hear the writers with no sense of time
The workshop writers, the Eastern boys
Dismiss a symphony in four dimensions
Compressed without loss and built
Of words and scent and time and rhyme
As mystic.

The Harper

2001

A night from which a freezing rain descended
Reached out for me in a dim-lit room,
Ticking on the windows,
      clicking on a dripping loom
Of drying grape vines clinging to the wall.

      Ireland was a trill,
      A run of fingers along strings
      Existing in the things played, things sung, songs.

And I remembered Babylon,
And Aughrim, and the Boyne.
Because the songs had brought me there,
Years before I breathed
      a churchyard air,
And read "*Cast a cold eye*" chiseled on a stone.

A Dog Doesn't Wonder

2013

A dog doesn't wonder if what he sees is real.
How happy is the dog.
The singer celebrates the rightness of the song.
How happy is the lyricist.
A man cares nothing for the soul.
How happy is that man.
The dog runs smiling to his fate.
How fortunate the dog.

9

Black Pool

2002

Dance: the light strikes water.
Ernst Haas and Lucien Clergue's
Friend, Picasso,
Evoked some ancient satisfaction;
Alfred Sisley, Alfred blue and gold.

      Returning down the beach near sundown
      With a green turtle dripping
      Grass basketful of oysters
      Young women with hard hands from gathering
      Stilled by the edge of sundown.

The dancing light mutating, leaving
An imprint on the cold mechanics
Of biology, a light impression,
On *cels d'argent* the macromemory
Of diamond bays, sand, and water.

      Thick the bodhrán taps the coming nightfall
      Timing the lapping of the surf,
      Contrapuntal to the sun's impression
      And bringing down to me the catchthroat
      Of light on water,
      Moved and only guessing why.

An Agincourt Trefoil

Agincourt One

Daylight! One-eyed, staring at the clouds;
Pressure at my nock, tension all along.
Straightened fibers, gray goose pennons tremble.

Made for this. Eager; frightened? Anxious.
Coming up now, pointing. The tension,
The pressure, release! I can't ... oh!

This is godly. Up. Out. Together,
All of us, hundreds together,
Dark above, below, and shouting
The war cry of the gray goose wing.
We fly, we live, we are at the center ... God!
What struck me?

Dark, buried in. Shaft shivered,
Splinters rushing past. Dark, warm, wet,
Flowing stains the gray goose wing.
Toppling on me, burying me,
Driving me into the mud,
And the warm wet everywhere.
What have I struck?
What have I done?

Agincourt Two

Damp and dirt on clothing
Are always most apparent to your hands.
Wet gloves with sand brought inside by wet fingers
Are uncomfortable,
Especially under chain mail.

And a blade that hasn't been kept
As scrupulously clean the last few days
As it should have been,
Made as free of rust by polishing with dry sand
As it would have been
If there'd been any dry sand to use,
Grates as it's drawn.

It's a feeling
Not so much a sound.
It reminds you that you're cold
And wet, and you haven't eaten
Since yesterday at noon.
Nothing spoils a victory like rain.

Agincourt Three

I slept last night in this shed.
The roof leaked, and the swine
Who claimed to own it
Required frightening off,
Like most of these Norman dogs.

Then, when I had just closed my eyes,
A man-at-arms, one of the nobility, *soi-disant,*
Stumbled in and demanded food.
He'd lost his sword and thrown away,
Most like, his breastplate and his helm.

His mail shirt, too, was missing,
And one of his gauntlets.
He had a scratch
On one cheek, but no more wound
Than that, as far as I could tell.

I looked him up and down,
Spat once in the straw, and
Showed him my baselard,
Said that was all the meal he'd get from me.
He swore, called me a name, and went back out.

I was not impressed.
One of the knights, he must have been,
The hangers-on of d'Albret or some lesser man,
The ones who rode over us in their haste
To get at the English.

I saw them go by, knocking we despised footmen
Left and right. Then they stuck, jammed against
The fools who'd preceded them.
The English were all on foot, those I saw,
But try to get one of our mountebanks to dismount.

When I saw our mighty crew of cowards
Began to turn and struggle to ride off, one fell
Heavily, just ahead of me.
I dropped my arbalest and started forward,
Thinking I'd take his purse or even get his sword.

But two English archers beat me there.
One hit him with the mallet they carry
To hammer in their sharpened stakes.
The other finished him with an axe.
And I, seeing more of them on the way, ran off.

Now I'm alive and many others aren't.
I'm unhurt, thank the devil, and only cold.
But my crossbow's lying somewhere on the field,
Or taken already by someone as light-fingered
As myself. Without it, I'm no one's man.

So when the sun's come up far enough
To show me east,
I'll face it, turn right, and walk south.
I have a little bread, half a head of garlic,
A few coins, and my knife.

If I skirt the towns,
Avoid the fleeing horsemen, and frighten away these
Bastard, villainous, northern peasants
When they think they can molest me,
I may see Gascony again.

An Individual Obsession

1988

"When thin Suger hurried toward the Seine"
Guillaume Apollinaire
"What a lot of weeping there was south of the Loire."
Pierre Leuliette

If you hear in the count of bells a drum
And sense in raspberry light of old rose windows
Or in the *Sainte Chapelle* a sunset you were denied,
Who am I to wonder? If silk robes of cardinals,
If popes' rings, kissed well enough, raised
Stone wonders for you, who am I to bring up plagues?

Crusades; Beziers, burnt Cathars;
A Mayan codex burning at the hands of damned,
Pig-ignorant priests − water under the dam.

If you'd rather breathe the air
Of 1110 AD, by all means, breathe.
Cast backward glances at the processional,
Drift off to sleep imagining the censors swinging,
Abbé Suger creating monuments by candlelight.
It's an innocent passion; there aren't that many left.
Consider where my own direction lies.
You could mention Stanleyville, the Congo,
Bomb shelters in suburbia; the butchers of Algiers.

You could ask what draws my eye
Backward to the post-war years, what makes me wish
That I was thirty then when the beast was fresh and
Clear-defined, when you could see exactly
What was to be destroyed, and enjoy the luxury
Of being wholly wrong,
Crouching in the jungle with a Swedish K.

Sessions   *1990*

Any horns out there?
Said the piano player.
Lots of players here tonight,
It's a session night,
And it sure is cold outside.

Got a good friend of mine
Here with his bass,
Here's a face you gonna get to know
Gonna ask a friend of mine
To come on up and sing a song.

Hey, man, go get your horn.
You bring your horn?
Lots of good players here tonight,
And I'm the only one gettin' paid.
They're all puttin' it up here for free,
Playin' for you, just for fun.

We're gonna take a short break,
Remember your waitress.
We'll be right back,
Lots of players here tonight,
And it sure is cold outside.

Passing By

Five-by-seven and a three-by-five,
What my mother used to call a four-in-hand,
Two-by-four make you feel alive.
North-by-northwest,
Step-by-step,
Swear-by-God, down by the strand.

Down by the banks of Cairnie,
We'll watch the small fish glide.
The Two-Hearted shore is stormy.
Eight-by-ten
On a two-by-twelve
Two by two, we'll take the ride.

In the Hospital

When you're in the hospital
Your goals contract and become tactical.

You forget 'learn Gaelic',
'Move to Sicily',
And 'finish the book'.

Instead, you focus on getting through
The next two sleepless hours
And ordering breakfast,
Walking ten feet,
And being discharged.

And so it comes as a surprise
To find family and friends,
Doctors and nurses,
Residents and interns and techs
Are worried that you'll die.

Federico Garcia Lorca *1998*

In July, the fresh green here begins to dust.
The spring's lushness loses its edge,
And the mound-shaped stands of sumac
Begin to look less tropical than they did in June.

Were there oleanders, Federico, in the bone yard?
In July, when the last faces you saw
Floated above black collars –
The murderers of your friends?

Old father lizard, who could read
The *Spanish Civil Guard* and forget?
What good is a massacre to history
Without its poet or its painter?

What can we find in genocidal excess,
What in brutal revolt without the love
Of a chronicle, without a masterwork,
Without image life to enjoin the dead?

So how about it ...
Could you and Gene Smith write a book?
Las Cantigas de San Pablo;
A major motion picture by Bunuel;
The heartless occurrence of silver cells;
The cross torn diagonal of a Spanish woman
Pulling thread; langoustines, paella,
And the bloody sand;
And the metronomic ticking of the sun and night.

Could you write of the conquest of Mexico?
Could you describe the hissing arc
The torch made as it passed
From Hapsburg hands to Hanover?
Could you sing for us the Spanish songs
That England learned and taught to Europe and to us?
The hopeless lays of empire and the hymns
Of those it leaves behind.

Even here, Federico, in some July,
We may stand in that same graveyard
Or under a globe of locust trees
While the summer buzzes and ...

Temptation and Revision   *1989*

I have played the games here in this café and
Across the plaza under the arch where the noon sun
Is cut to black shadow in just such a way,
Marching precisely closer to the center of the street
Each noon for half each year, then marching back.

Here in my provincial town, I've seen the games.
I know the players, and I understand each man,
His depth and breadth and level of commitment.
I have been an ideologue although
A woman's face, or voice,
Or long, dark hair has once or twice ...

> Still in Chile
> It's come down to this.
> "Please, Señor Augusto, go away."
> A plebiscite on outrage,
> Voting against the devil.

And Mao and Marx are little help; Vo Nguyen Giap
Is strangely silent on these terms, and even
These bitter manuals we brought from the north
Seem sapped, somehow, in strength,
Here in this eternal day.
The sun soaks itself in our café.

So now it's time, I think, to go
As I've so often thought of going.
Bits of paper stained with rum
Are all the leave-behind I leave;

Bits of wood and steel the coming-to.
Behind: the hours, the talk, the rest of you.

Here in the plaza or even from the market gate
We cannot see the mountains. There it waits
Behind that first green line of hills;
Clear and well defined, exonerating death.
An end of dialectic and a way to say, "At last ..."

After the Funeral

2004

I sat down with Wilfred Owen
With the angular sun beams
In our great room
And the glowing vine leaves in the window.

Looking up, I saw a small statue
My own father made
In dark wood
Of a sailor standing watch.

Some friend had moved him up
High onto the windowsill
Safe from children,
And his binoculars looked straight at me.

I raised my cup of strong coffee
À santé, Bon Père, I said.
Welcome another sailor
A man you scarcely knew, laid aside today.

The two of you were not at all alike
Except you sailed in the same war
Under the same flag
And wanted handsome things for those around you.

You were both loved greatly, missed,
And will be missed,
À santé, Bon Père,
To both of you, I raised the cup again.

Growing Uncaring

Lately I find
That I don't give one single flying damn
For the things that keep you up at night
And make you fly those banners on your car.

Katie, I knew
You always drifted to the right
And I just let it go.
Now it's gone too far.

You talk of sin.
Well, here's a sin for you:
Telling and believing lies.
Katie, on that score you're bound for hell.
You are not well.
There's a dead look in your eyes
That's something new.

When we first met
There was no talk of hosts
Or holy ghosts.
No china angels on the shelf;
You could enjoy yourself.

When I hear you talk
About the wicked left,
I'm never sure
What you think those people did to you.
Or is it just that they don't care,
And you so want them to.

26

You're old enough to know –
You went to school –
There is no single Tao,
No gods, no heavens, and no hell
Except the ones you make yourself.
You used to do that well.
You didn't need the righteous boys
To tell you how.

Now your friends are those
I do not nod to on the street.
I hate to be this way,
But I refuse to meet
Zealous bastards of the kind
Who lied the children into war
Twice before.
They're just not worth the time;
I might be indiscreet.

So Katie, you must pick and choose
Which one you lose,
Those lies or me.
What you believe
Is not just false but wrong,
And you are no longer free.

So you go on ahead.
Me, I'm headed for the bar.
Such a dark and quiet holy place
Where my old cronies are
And any lessons to be learned
Are not received but earned.

Marriage Equality Referendum, Ireland   *2015*

The children racing, elders embracing,
The bright-eyed men, the bright young women,
Racing to place the question, and
To force an answer,
Tracing a wider line than before
Between then and now.

While Gaia goes unworshipped, and,
Unbridled and untamed,
The old church and the new ones stand, and
The dark and narrow foreheads
Of tightlipped men go unshamed,
How can anyone who simply loves another one
Be blamed?

Mount your guard, remember
In your yard and in your house and on your quiet couch,
How close a thing a race can be.
To live freely and stay free, recall all
The days and nights you fought.
Fix your armor, store away the things you bought,
Patch your tattered coat,
And remember *Home to Vote.*

UPS *2016*

Brown-clothed djinn
With his noisy caravan
Brings goods from far away
No longer sold here in the bazaar.
How my dog hates him.

He brings obscure writings
To my palace door,
Certain kinds of raiment,
Magic wands to charm,
And turn, and form the world.
But how my dog hates him.

Leader Dog Blues

2013

Wake up in the morning,
She puts my red vest on.
Wake up in the morning,
I get my red vest on.
Pick up the harness, mama,
We're down the street and gone.

I'm a leader, baby, I'm a leader dog.
I'm a born leader, baby, I'll lead you anywhere.
I'll steer you through the traffic,
And I will get you there.

We go down the subway,
And we ride that train.
We go down the subway,
Waitin' for the train.
Go shoppin' for the groceries,
And we come home again.

Nappin' in the sunlight,
Rest my head upon her knee.
Nappin' on the sofa,
My head is restin' on her knee.
I'm just a leader dog, baby,
That's how it is with me.

Neither drink nor feasting   *2017*

The life you live's unsatisfactory,
Always watching, unrewarding
But in dross and tarnished coinage,
Stamped with antique names and faces
Of men you don't remember,
Men you never knew.

> And neither drink nor feasting
> Will ban the dark *Erinyes*
> Or the shame of being human
> From your mind.

The children you engendered
Unregarding, unregarded,
And angry little creatures,
No more your own creation
Than the country they were born in:
You've neither made nor shaped them
Nor yourself.

And the more you try for visions,
Put your fingers where you shouldn't,
And believe without a reason,
The less you are rewarded
In the early morning hours
With answers even close to seeming sane.

Now you've made a flaming blunder.
Like the dozens made before it,
This one rests upon your pillow
In the red and violent smoking,
Shocked and shattered morning
Of the day you cease to be.

>And neither drink nor feasting
>Could mute the dark *Erinyes*
>Or keep the shame of being human
>From your mind.

Replacing a tree

2016

A short, brittle, deciduous shrub,
Here when we bought the place,
Was finally winter killed.

I am no more a man who
Cuts down trees or digs large holes.
We bought an evergreen
And had it delivered and installed.

The man who came was
1970 itself,
Paper-white beard and long hair,
Black wrap-around sunglasses;
My age, give or take a few.

In twenty minutes he was done,
Old tree gone, new spruce in place.
"I won't charge you for removal,"
He said. "Didn't take any time at all.
Take care, now."

When was the last time a man
Your own age made you feel old?

The Stone Boat

2017

Shiawassee County Images

So, growing up, you didn't have one?
A kind of sled
With a flat bottom. No runners.
They'd just break
Under the weight of the stones or cement blocks
You throw onto it so you
Can haul them away.

The one I remember was one
My father made. A sheet of
Galvanized iron
Sledge-hammered into
Shape like a punt.

What's a punt? Come on.
Everybody knows that.
We had one of those, too.
A real boat to go on water.
Flat-bottomed
With blunt ends.

A stone boat, though,
Goes on land. Dragged behind
A tractor or a Jeep. I saw one once
Made from the hood of a car.

Hide and Go Find

Rain on my cheek,
Theory of mind.

Not a comfort or a plan
For the younger conscience
Still scanning the horizon,
Looking over the shoulder,
Learning as a means to an end,
By rote.

Rather a choice for an older brain
Making up for lost time,
Finally knowing what some allusion means,
How an algorithm works,
Who the writer was, and why
He wrote.

Ceasing to seek,
Starting to find.

One Evening

2017

The same sky, the same blue space,
Mottled today with high white,
Last night was pale gray and duotone
As atmospheric stone.
The valley wall, half a mile of lake away,
Was grayed
By rain into a scribbled skyline,
Like a long mound of
Gray-green grain.

One late boat, wet on both sides,
Left only a dark wake
On the surface of the lake
To quickly dissipate;
The current stayed to keep
A few dark streaks
On the same silver face
Of the water as it moved.
Outside, a table top,
Already slick and wet,
Sent back in spatters
Excess drops of rain.

A sparrow rushed past.
The cedar branches scarcely moved,
And only the Scots pine's needles
Were fine enough to move with the rain,
And nothing mattered
But the rain.

This morning, there's fog.
From the surface of the lake
To a hint of blue at the highest point.
The fog shuts all out impenetrably.
Copiously the wet soil gives up moisture
And closes off the valley.
Sight ends with a cedar's tangle
Half the width of the house
And beyond it, just the light gray
Of the coming day.

Within an hour, the fog
Gives way to clarity,
Sun on water,
Blue above and below,
And variegated greens
Along the valley wall.
The several things that mattered
Recently, give way
And nothing matters,
A little or at all.

Business Cards

2017

I never had one job for long.
Always a change in title or
In company
Moved me along,
And I never in thirty years
Used up one box
Of business cards.

Some I threw out,
Others saved,
Who knows why.
Now a dozen lie
On the table
By my reading chair.
Lying there, they make
Perfect bookmarks.

The Old Man Himself

For thirty years next year
The Old Man will have been gone.
Not father, not dad, just Mac.
No one I knew ever called him James.

Intensely patient,
So silent around the house that
I could never imagine him teaching,
Which he did for forty years.

So unimaginably capable
That he could take five summers
And an existing, derelict foundation,
And build by himself the house I grew up in.

I have his work, the corpus of his painting
And his printmaking,
And his Emeritus certificate,
A bit water-stained and mouse-nibbled in one corner.

I know that a fifteenth-century relative
On Mac's mother's side
Was a Sheriff of Nottingham.
I know that Mac had friends who died fighting fascists in Spain.

I know he helped with antiaircraft guns
On a merchant ship in the Italian landings,
And that he was shipwrecked
Off Martha's Vineyard in a storm.

I know what his art consisted of;
Some of it hangs on my wall, here.
I can see some influences
Of the Cubists in the earlier work.

But I don't know a damned thing
About the old man himself.

<u>**Songs**</u>

These pieces were composed over a long period of time, usually, before ever being written down.

A Holiday Anthem   *2009*

It snowed throughout December
More than I remember
       Now it's Christmas Eve
       And it's forty degrees
Happy Holidays in Michigan.

Melting mounds of gray and brown
Are strewn around our little town
       Skies are gray
       Gonna stay that way
Happy Holidays in Michigan.

Just cold enough to need a coat
Cough and sneeze and clear your throat
       Everyone complains
       Tell me that isn't rain
Happy Holidays in Michigan.

It's safer here than someplace coastal
But everyone I know is postal
       Ain't sentimental
       Makes me mental
Happy Holidays in Michigan.

Marches, camps, and Empire

2016

You know that I had rather been a singer,
You know that I would rather play the horn.
You know I'd fancy playin' on the fiddle.
But to marches, camps, and empire I was born.

My father was a boy who fed the horses.
My mother was a daughter of the sea.
When the fever came to Benares by the river,
All it left were sorrow, want, and me.

A sergeant found me sleepin' in a feed box.
He gave me to his childless wife to raise.
Now it's I who wear the musket on my shoulder.
I guess that I will wear it all my days.

But even so the nights when I was lyin'
Upon the ground, my pack beneath my head.
The music came and always sent me dreamin'
Of other roads and where they might have led.

And now we're back in barracks here in Dublin,
And it's pints around at Jimmy's down the street.
I sing my songs of marches, camps, and Empire,
And bring these drunken bastards to their feet.
        And I bring these drunken bastards to their feet.

42

Proceedings Set to Waltz Time

2015

My eyes are sore
From the air conditioned air
And from having to stare
At words on a screen
      Twenty feet away.

Six hours ago
We knew this wouldn't go.
That dog won't hunt,
      And the answer is no.

But still we're talking,
And no one's balking,
But what do the users want?
      Words to and fro.

And now we're done
We didn't do
      anything
But time is
      On the wing.
And we thank everyone.

Now we're leaving the room

And returning our calls

As the evening falls

      And the pay's the same, anyway.

      And the pay

           Is the same,

                Anyway.

Stories

That's what these are: stories, short, long, and all that.

Antiquities   *2017*

Given the nature of the place, I expected the security to be tighter. In fact, it probably was, but I remember hearing from an old Courts and Law reporter that the best security is the thing you don't notice. I also expected a more imposing public interface – okay, entrance – than I found. I did have to show my appointment confirmation to a gate guard, but then it was just a matter of parking in a "visitor" space.

The front door wasn't locked or card-controlled, and the lobby was small. The woman at the desk looked properly official. She had a green-gray uniform, with a peaked cap lying next to a very standard-looking keyboard and screen setup. She herself was professionally open and cheerful.

"Good morning. Are you Anne O'Connor?" she asked, and I said yes, I was. "From the *Journal*, I think? Here to see ... " she looked at her screen "... Major Awara?" Again, I confirmed. "I'll let her know you're here." She tapped briefly on her keyboard and said that my press contact officer would be right with me.

There were a couple of upholstered chairs, and I sat down. I hadn't adjusted the rental car's seat properly, and my back hurt from the drive. Given the mission of this place, I thought, their lobby appointments seem ... ironic. There were a couple of happy pictures – pointless landscape acrylics – the chairs, a door behind the receptionist, and nothing else. I couldn't see any, but I took it for granted there were cameras.

Major Awara showed up almost at once, as advertised . She wore the same unpatterned uniform, no cap, and a sidearm of some kind in a webbing holster. As she showed me through the door, I glanced at the desk person and saw that she was armed, too.

We went a short way down a corridor and into a small meeting room. It had the inevitable conference table and chairs, but also a pair of armchairs with a side table between. Awara waved me to them. "It's just the two of us today," she said. "Colonel Brooke can't join us, unfortunately." She offered coffee or water, but I don't do that on interviews. I don't like to begin by accepting anything except cooperation-within-reason.

I thanked her for meeting with me, and I explained that I was one of probably dozens of journalists doing stories on the CDA, now that it had emerged from its initial clandestine status. I said that I'd want an overview of its mission, some idea of sizes and other statistics, and a few specific examples of the work it does. That would be the kick-off, I said, for a series of in-depth stories, running over the next six months or so. Although I knew the very basic idea of the agency, I said that she should assume I really knew nothing at all.

She nodded. "Happy to do that. As you say, there are a lot of questions about us, and you're actually only the second person I've talked to."

"Would you mind telling me who else has been in touch?" I asked. She demurred and began with a standard-sounding spiel.

"Let's start with the absolute basics. CDA, of course, is the Cultural Defense Agency. We're an international group, nominally reporting to the Secretary General of the United Nations. Practically, we're under the direct command of the United States Department of Defense and similar organizations in the European Community."

"Where does the funding come from?" I asked.

"Three general sources." She ticked off three fingers. "Penalties from violators. Base levels of funding from virtually all countries. Fees from museums, universities, and other cultural institutions."

"What supplies the funding from countries?"

"That's up to the countries. In the US, for example, it's a budget line item."

"Taxes, that is?"

"Yes, taxes. Some of the smaller countries get parts of their contribution waived in return for cooperating with us. With enforcement."

That I'd already heard. "Again," I said, "some of this is already public, but list for me the categories of things you protect."

"Of course. Human artifacts on any scale. Specimens of extinct or rare species. Of anything, basically, including humans. Specific precious metals and minerals. Works of art and architecture."

"I want to come back to architecture in a minute," I said, "but confirm for me that specimens means living or dead examples of animals, living things?"

"Yes, it does. And if I can anticipate you, yes it includes examples of individual human remains. Certain examples. Not all, of course."

"So ancestral remains or remains that a tribe believes are ancestral — you cover those?"

"Not all. Remains that have already been returned — given back to a group — aren't covered. We don't go and dig them up again. But human remains earlier than a specific date — 500 BCE — that are newly discovered or still held by institutions — those are in our jurisdiction."

"Hmm. Has that been controversial, at all?"

"It's varied. The problems, issues, concerns, they vary with the specific cases. Since we have separate national and regional divisions, each one has its own constituents, and the concern varies with the amount of remaining ... religious feeling. Some groups don't care, some do."

"Let's leave that for the moment. Tell me about cultural objects. Why are you involved, what's being done, what's the reaction?"

"First, let me answer the what are they? question. What do we mean by cultural objects? We use that term to cover anything a human culture created, restricted by a set of criteria. Those criteria are constructed to measure the value in cultural terms, not in economic terms."

"I know this won't be a short answer, but how on earth do you do that? Separate economics from culture?"

"We started — and the measures are intended to grow and change over time — by leaving market forces absolutely out. We don't care at all how much money a wealthy person would pay to own an object. We assess the contribution the object makes to an existing culture. Imagine a Hindu statue, for example. Hinduism still exists, and people worship at the place where the statue was. Next, we look at the object's contribution to understanding. Mesopotamian religions aren't practiced today, but an artifact related to them makes a contribution to our understanding of that bygone culture. And last, we measure the threat to the object itself. For non-living objects, we see really only two threats: theft and destruction."

"Wait," I said. "Theft and destruction? That's all?"

"Destruction covers a lot of ground. In our terms, it doesn't have to be total. If you spray-paint your name on a building, you partly destroy it. Both with your act and with the changes in the surface that occur when the paint is removed. You didn't tear down the building, but you partly destroyed it."

"And those assessments? They make some kind of score or measure ...?"

47

"Yes. And if the score is higher than a set of thresholds, the object comes into our control."

"That brings me to the why question." I stretched, trying to get the kink in my back to go away. "But before that, can we take a quick break? Are there restrooms handy?"

"Of course. Just go out the door here, and they're right where the hall ends."

"And I don't need a badge or ... an escort? To wander around?"

"No. From this part of the site, people can't get anywhere near storage or lab space."

While I was using the facilities, I thought of another question. How about rarity? A thing is old, sure, but say there are hundreds of examples already known and secure. Does that make it less threatened? What if it's naturally perishable? Lots of animal parts get used in traditional medicine. How would that work with the three criteria? But first, that *why* issue. I knew some of the unofficial answers, but I had to hear the official one first.

Back in the conference room, the Major went ahead with the reason her agency existed. "The core problem, the thing that made it necessary for the CDA to be formed, was REPS. Rapid Economic and Population Shifts. Five years ago, a group of social researchers discovered, well, they discovered each other. They found that work was being done on some similar issues, all over the developed world. They agreed to join their teams and try to identify more groups working on the same basic question. They called it the subtle impacts question: what are the less obvious effects of human population expansion?"

"Okay," I said, "That's a term we've heard. And the REPS consortium – REPSCO – that, too. But I have to admit, it didn't seem like something that would really kick off global action."

"True. And it actually didn't, by itself. But one of the themes they identified was taken up by universities, and they agreed that they'd – to use a crude phrase – rub their governments' noses in it."

"Really?"

"Yes. The theme they brought to the table, many tables, actually, was wealth growth impact. Simply put, more wealth was accumulating in more hands, and the new hands weren't under any kind of control."

"I thought wealth was concentrating in a few hands?"

"In the sense of magnitude of wealth, yes. But below that one or two percent, the next tier down is also expanding. And for much of that segment, it's new wealth."

"All right, but what about control? What do you mean by control?"

"Restraint is probably a better word. The effect that REPSCO saw was an increasing demand for irreplaceable things. Art, architecture, artifacts, fossils, anatomical specimens. And the demand was to have them for the sake of having them, not to expand knowledge, not to study, not to provide insight, but just to have them."

"That doesn't seem like a breathtakingly new insight, if you'll pardon me saying so. The phrase "nouveau riche" comes to mind."

"For the record, you used that term, not me."

"Okay. But what about traditional medicine, say? Animal species being killed for just a specific body part?"

"It's not that the demand is new, it's the scale. And the emergence of what's being called MEDEM – manufactured emotional demand. Simply, fake news: dried, powdered aardvark liver pitched as a virility drug. Traditional has become a code word for something the greedy oppressor doesn't want you to know about. As in, a thing was invented yesterday by three men over coffee, but there wasn't any law against calling it traditional."

"I see. And this isn't new, but the size of it is? Oh, and of course, the damage it does?"

"Yes. That's what CDA was founded to combat."

"That's ... ambitious. A really big job. And you see the problem as the whole effect of animal trafficking, art theft, illegal ... metal detector hobbyists? All of that?"

"That's right. All of that."

"And ... um, I have to ask: how's that working out for you?"

"You're sitting in one of our facilities, the US operations headquarters. We have 2,450 employees in the US. 400 of them, give or take, are here. Around the world, the average is 1,600 staff per member country, and 1.6 locations. Together, we've written model legislation, and helped 19 countries tailor it. Of those, 17 have passed their laws, and the rest will become law in the next two years."

"I had no idea."

"Most of the staff work is in enforcement, preservation, and curation. There are two manufacturing centers, one here and one in Zurich. Their people are the fourth big group. Beyond that, there's a much smaller set of people like me, our legal teams, and our government relations experts. And of course, a handful of general management."

"Manufacturing?"

"Yes. We can't keep people from seeing things, studying them, after all. Just because they're endangered."

"That's amazing This is ... bigger than I would have imagined. But what really astounds me is your being able to keep it under the radar for this long. Why was that necessary? Why are you and I talking now, not, oh, three years ago?"

"I have to answer this carefully. The reason is that part of the MEDEM phenomenon is a systemic resistance to outside control. The entities who supply cultural objects illegally are like living beings: they evolve to meet environmental pressure. Ivory poaching was unstructured to begin with. Countries reacted to it by creating armed warden teams. The poachers reacted by becoming armed groups themselves, and because they were supplying a wealth-driven demand, they were able to become better-armed than the poachers."

"Right. Individual journalists and activists are targets. I see that."

"And so CDA had to get its people and assets and laws in place carefully and quietly, then go into operation quickly and in many places at once. A species that's threatened by gradual desertification has time to adapt to a dry environment. A meteorite collision doesn't allow enough time for evolution to work."

"I bet I could find some holes in that example, but I see your point. And, so besides uniform law templates, what does CDA actually do?"

"We operate the World Wide Safe Havens network." She swept her hand around. "This is one. We lead national cultural law enforcement teams. And probably the most important thing: we supply the Enhanced Facsimiles."

"Facsimiles of what? The things you protect?"

"Yes, exactly."

"I get the manufacturing now. So you're busy. I understood the cultural law part, I think. And safe havens ... like museums? The facsimiles, though. That's got to be ... immense!"

"It is. But let's take things one at a time. First, the Safe Havens aren't exactly museums. They're designed to preserve cultural objects for as long as it's physically possible. Access to the LOs ... oh, did I cover that term? It means Literal Object. An actual thing that is of cultural contribution and under threat. So the LOs aren't on display to the public. They don't get loaned to museums, shipped around among our facilities, and never, of course, sold to anybody. They're kept in a single Safe Haven, permanently."

"No one gets to study them?"

"Oh, yes, certainly. But researchers have to demonstrate that their work requires access to an LO, and that the research is absolutely non-destructive. Whatever they do with the LO has to be done in the Safe Haven, using equipment we own, and it has to leave the LO exactly as it is."

"And when you say "researchers", you mean ...?"

"Degreed, credentialed primary investigators, representing an accredited research institution. Once an LO comes under our jurisdiction, it loses any religious or traditional associations, except, again, for credentialed researchers."

Lord, I thought. I'd heard this hinted at, but not in this somewhat totalitarian light. I suddenly understood why the whole effort was kept under wraps until the legal framework was ready.

"What I think you just described ... does it imply that if you have my great-grandfather's skull in here as an LO, I can't come and visit it?"

"Yes. If you can get a credentialed anthropologist, specializing in the time and place where your grandfather lived, and if she can present a convincing research program that requires 3D imaging of osteological specimens, she could have access to it and give you the logic file to 3D print an exact replica. But not you, unless you can establish those credentials yourself."

"Given that, why would any researcher cooperate with you?"

"I mentioned that we have many people in enforcement? The legal packages the member countries pass require one or more of our people to be in the field, keeping track of what's being discovered. No observer, no permit. The observers also go into museums and other public sites. To inventory and assess the contribution of objects, and any threats to them."

"But ... are you saying that 19 countries agree that putting things out of sight is ... justifiable? What about museums? Galleries? Cathedrals? Plain old monuments? For that matter, what about structure of existing buildings? How ...?"

"That's always the big question. And now that we're operating openly, we have to answer it as clearly as we can. Let's start with moveable LOs."

"What, paintings and idols and so on?"

"Yes. Things that can be transported to a Safe Haven. I mentioned that manufacturing was one of our four large divisions? They make absolutely accurate Surrogate Objects: SOs. And they provide them to the original holder at no charge. Other institutions can acquire SOs at a charge. They are, as far as the viewer's experience is considered, identical. But they also have some additional properties."

"Like identification, I imagine."

"Exactly. Embedded microprocessors. They detect physical contact, movement, damage – even surface damage. And they self-identify, so nobody can pass one off as the real thing."

"This is giving me a headache. What about ... oh, I don't know ... animal parts?"

"We don't inventory more than a few examples of any biological LO. When rhino horn is seized, we only keep a sample and destroy the rest."

"Christ. But ... buildings? You don't keep whole cathedrals? Or bridges from Venice?"

"No, although small pieces of architectural materials, we do. With larger LOs, we leave them in situ, but use a rapid 3D imaging system, inside and out. We can create virtual copies when they're needed, and it's just the reverse of other LOs; that data is available to anyone, along with software to use it."

"But are you saying that you're going to do ... do everything? Anything that might be stolen or damaged or ..."

"Well, no. I should have made that clear at the outset. I'll add that to my notes. I think I said that you're only the second journalist I've briefed."

"And you're still not going to tell me who the first one was, are you?"

"No, sorry. But I won't tell anyone else about you, either. So the SOs and the storage of LOs is only part of the picture. We make it hard to steal something of value and easy to prove that one of our surrogates isn't where it should be. All that aspect of things. But it doesn't do a threatened

52

species any good to secure their bits of anatomy, after they've been killed. I think I mentioned preservation as one of our divisions?"

"Yes."

"Preservation is actually a military organization. Of the member nations, only the US, France, and Germany provide people and technology, and they're never stationed in their home countries. The Foreign Legion wasn't really a model, but it underlies the design."

"The Foreign Legion?"

"Just in concept. Enforcement that's at least one step removed from local ... entanglements."

"And I can guess, but they do what, exactly?"

"They stop the supply of LOs at the point of origin. We can't take all the whales and put them in an aquarium, but we can make the oceans a safe place for them to be."

"But ... how?"

"There are two elected officials and 23 citizens of an East Asian country serving long jail sentences now. And four whaling ships were seized in the last year."

"You're taking ships? Stopping and boarding ships?"

"We have two frigates contributed by India and one from Australia. Working in the Pacific. Just in the Pacific."

"Holy ... I guess I'll find out in the next day or so who else you've briefed. But don't you think ... isn't this just a bit new-world-order?"

"How do mean?"

"What about the people ... criminals, maybe, but still people who make a living on all this stuff?" *Stuff?* I thought. Did I really say all this *stuff* in an interview question? My back hurt, and my head was beginning the regular throb that lack of caffeine brings on.

"None of the member countries recognize a human right to exploit resources outside of defined limits. In evolution, a group of members of a species that begins to exploit a hazardous niche− one that decreases their chance of reproducing − can't expect to be spared the consequences of making that choice. What the CDA's enforcement group is, essentially, is a human-designed environmental force. It exists to make sure that choosing to do cultural exploitation is evolutionarily disadvantageous."

"Let me draw a long breath here," I said. "This is ... a bigger story than I imagined. To put it mildly. What about ... what about currently-produced art works? If I paint a picture tomorrow, does that automatically go into the system? How do I get compensated for creating that work?"

"Remember that we assess contribution and threat. If you paint something one day, it's not likely to make a contribution to understanding your culture on the next day. It might be under threat — you caricatured the President or offended some ethnic group — but again, until it's exhibited, displayed, exposed to risk, we can't evaluate threat. No offense intended, but the mass of cultural objects being produced today really doesn't say much about our culture, except in its massiveness. So the inclusion of individual paintings, sculpture, advertising ... for one reason or another, they'll never generate a contribution and threat score sufficient to come into our scope." She paused while I took notes. "At least not for a length of time."

She went on. "There are, of course, current artists whose work may need protection. There's a central, data-driven, risk-assessment committee that monitors the rise of art and artists, worldwide. For example, there's a young woman in the Ukraine who was essentially unknown until last year. Then she started to become noteworthy after one of the border incidents with Russia became the subject of a statue she made. Threats against it — and against her, incidentally — started to appear, and so we added her statue to the threatened list. Here, let me show you." She had a notepad computer with her, and she'd apparently anticipated this topic.

"This is the real statue, and there's an SO in the original square where the real one stood. Within a month, the surrogate had been attacked twice by Russian supporters. All but one of them were caught, since detection imaging capabilities were built into the SO."

"But did the artist benefit from the protection?"

"Yes, she was paid a fee, amounting to 12% of the money she'd already been paid by the city for the original piece."

"Amazing. And you got all this into legal codes in, what did you say, 17 countries?"

"Two more are in the process."

"My God. I can't believe your first interview hasn't published yet."

"Well, I talked to him just yesterday."

"Still ... Oh, wait. How about this? What about endangered artists, themselves? The Ukrainian lady; her work is protected, but what about her, herself?"

"That isn't in our charter, sadly. There are other organizations, though. They provide both health and life insurance for threatened creatives. In fact, there appears to be a kind of pressure from these carriers applied to governments. It's in the carriers' interest to damp down hostile actions and threats, keeping their exposure down."

"Yes, I'd heard a bit about that. But no specifics. Do you know any examples?"

"It's not my area of expertise, but there were rumors last year that a carrier had protection policies on both certain Russian officials and on some people in Chechnya, and the insurers were able to keep both sets of clients alive by threatening to raise rates or even drop coverage if anything unpleasant happened."

"I don't think I'm cynical enough for all this. It's given me a headache," I complained.

"Oh, I'm sorry. Would you like to see some examples of SOs? There's an exhibit we're putting together here, just so we have something to demonstrate."

"Yeah, that would be nice."

"Come with me, then. We've got a Nike of Samothrace set up, and there are some hand axes from St. Acheul. As Colonel Brooke likes to say, they don't look a day over half a million years."

Doctor Erlen Meijer, he thought. *Adjunct Professor Doctor Erlen Meijer.* He picked up another book from a pile and put it with others in a box. A young man with a newly-published dissertation can expect to do a lot of moving, and Erlen was packing up his efficiency in Newport. Over the eight years he'd spent in one school or another, he'd acquired a facility for living lightly, making kits of essential gear, the cooking kit, the clothing kit, the technology kit. Instead of an old car, he had an eleven-year-old pickup truck with a cap over the bed. With that and a few reused boxes, he could move out of or into a small apartment in less than a day. Travel was likewise codified. When he had to fly, he took a backpack and a shoulder bag for his laptop. One went under the seat ahead and the other overhead. His residences were bare of decoration, but he was as ready to depart as a fugitive. The only flaw in the logistical schema was the books.

He was a literary academic, and the equipment of his profession was almost as bulky as that of a biologist or a physician. His dissertation discussed an obscure aspect of D. H. Lawrence and the New Mexico period. It was built, of course, on published material, and what Erlen saved by streamlining his physical life, he spent on books, journals, and reprints of articles. He kept track of things he had on hand, and he always referred to his list before he bought anything else. The list, at this point in his career, had 328 titles in one physical form or another, not to mention 204 digital documents. It occurred to him, usually late at night, that instead of coffee spoons, he'd measured out his life in volumes of literary criticism and technique.

Now, though, he was past two milestones. He'd completed his doctoral work and found an actual faculty job, and he was prepared to part with some of the library. The near term task was a move to Michigan, and over 30 of his old books were going into a box that would not be going with him. It would go only as far as an online sales service. Soon, these books, some well-used, some barely explored, would go back into circulation, and the few dollars he got for them would pay for some of the gasoline the drive would burn up.

He picked up a hardbound volume, a leftover from an undergraduate Humanities class. He realized that he'd been carrying it around ever since, without once referring to it. He was near the end of the culling and packing process, and he spared a moment to flip a few pages. He noticed at once that it was annotated. The sections that were covered in the course were covered in the book with notes in his handwriting, and he was first surprised and then amused at his early reactions to what the author had to say.

The book was Konstanza Eueler's *Surreal Film: The Narrative of Non-narration*. In his sophomore year, it had been *au courant* in film school circles, and Erlen had paid a little less than fifty dollars for a new copy. As it turned out, the reputation of the author and his interest in film waned at the same rate, but at the time, he'd worked his way through the book, carefully underlining things and writing, as he thought you were supposed to, things like "Wow!" or "Hmmm?" in the margin. As the text went on, his comments gained greater weight in his undergraduate self-estimation. He added references to other writers, even managing to bring Susan Sontag into it and inserting a gratuitous reference to the Catholic liturgy.

Today, as he read through it, he began to be embarrassed by what he'd thought of things, all those years back—or, he realized suddenly, by what he'd thought he was supposed to think, the not-insightful insights he'd borrowed, and the obvious pretension of it all. The gerund *posing* came to mind, and if he'd been familiar with it, so would the meme *imposter syndrome*. He closed the book with what was nearly a shudder, dropped it into the box, and folded the flaps. *Time to go.*

Eight years went by. Erlen was almost completely absorbed by his young career. Positions in the humanities were thin on the ground, and the amount of work, far removed from study and analysis, was by itself enough for a full job. On top of the departmental administrivia came teaching, counseling identity-crisis-stricken undergraduates, and always, always, the struggle to publish, present, and be noted. The quarterly accounting of funds and grants and stipends would have made Luca Pacioli hesitate.

The environments - the departments – were hierarchical in a way that nationalistic governments could only admire. Still a young and relatively new academic, Erlen existed in an environment of sweetly expressed passive aggression. The old joke about the psychiatrist who says "Good morning" and the colleague who thinks "I wonder what he meant by that?" was a remarkably apt touchstone. Erlen accepted it and even found a space within it. So, although each passing year made it harder to think about another way of making a living, he scraped out a tiny den in a shrinking wilderness. He wasn't aware of any serious failings or false steps or blots on his escutcheon. And so a discussion, one on one with his department Chair, was not unusual or especially frightening. Sitting across a desk from her, he nodded at the right times, offered a few suggestions he knew would be acceptable, and saw the clear signs of the meeting coming to an end. He stood up.

At this point, the Chair leaned back, thanked him, and then picked up a book. It was a hardcover, worn a bit at the edges of the binding, dark blue with white titles. "I can't stay out of book stores," she said. "I was in Atlanta this week, and I wandered into a place just off campus. I saw this, and I just had to have it. Very dated, of course. The text itself is funny enough, but the comments someone's written in it are a scream." She turned it around and pushed it across the deck. There, in text larger than the title, was *Konstanza Eueler.* The black and white picture of her, wearing a beret and standing in front of a pillared university building, struck Erlen like a swastika spray-painted on a door.

Oh my God, he thought. Every look, every slightly stiff greeting from the Chair, every laughing conversation he'd seen her have, far down a hall with someone else, appeared like captions on a screen. *My God, my God, did I write my name in that book?!*

He picked it up, opened it to the inside of the cover. No name there. He turned a few pages. "Oh, yes," he said. His mouth was exceedingly dry. "I ... I see what you mean." He pretended to look for more notes, scanning for anything that might give him away. "Oh. Oh, yes. I see. Very funny." He put it back on the desk, glanced desperately at his watch, and made some papier-mâché exit line.

All night, he was awake, turning over and over in his mind the ways that his childishness might be traced back to him. On one hand, he argued, *if she'd known, why would she have shown it to me? How could she know? And why would she want to confront me with it?* He tried to imagine something he might have done or said to offend. It wouldn't have to have been to her; *it could have been with someone else and they reported it.*

What are you saying? he'd ask. *What do you mean, 'reported' it? This isn't the Soviet Union. There's no KGB here.* But the memories kept coming back: the foolish, naive, self-assured youth he'd been and the callow, received ideas he'd betrayed. And then, near dawn, the real horror descended on him. *That was only one book!*

He could see, as clearly as if he were back in that Rhode Island apartment, the box of books. He drew in a deep breath as he realized that he'd deliberately selected things from his early years, purposefully gathered up titles in which he might have written *anything*! And if one obscure and long-forgotten piece of the 1980s had surfaced, where were the others? And in how many of them had he fatally recorded himself as an owner?

He got up, walked to the window of his bedroom, and raised the shade. Even in the dark, the shape of the town was laid out in streetlights. Up a hill, though, the university itself was a darker rectangle, framed in the external lines of bright roads. The reality of the situation closed in and made itself a comfortable home. This was a personal issue. All of the time spent learning, following, and relearning the rules, all of those uncomfortable meetings, interviews, starched-stiff social events, all of those petty, uninformed, cavalier comments from reviewers ... all that he'd endured to be here, clinging to a crack in the cliff face with just the edge of the summit of Mount Tenure visible ... all of that was at stake.

He turned around and went to the small second bedroom. There was a desk and his laptop was on it. In a couple of minutes, he was looking at his long book inventory list, sorting it by date acquired, and scrolling through to the items marked as "Sold". In a second window, he brought up a browser. One by one, he began working his way through the list of entries, searching used book sites. *How long will this take me,* he wondered, *and how much will I have to spend to destroy the evidence?*

The Assault on Cerro Roja

2016

by a Trooper of the 31ˢᵗ Battalion

Heads down. Officers say stay down. Staff will order rebels to surrender. No talk. Must surrender. Troopers lying behind a ledge. Rebels are up the hill. They make trenches, but small. Low, not as troopers would have made. Rebels had no time.

Staff shouting at rebels. No answer. Ears up. Listening carefully. No answer.

Somebody shoots! Not us. Maybe third battalion. On the left. Not us. Maybe rebels. More shots. Ears down. Officer says down! Guns start shooting from behind. Big guns on the left, with the third battalion. Our mortars shooting, too. Rebels' trench is torn up. Dirt flying. Smoke and noise. We are all head down. Some shooting back and forth. Not much. Rebels hiding.

Officers say attention! Prepare! Big guns stop. Third battalion's bugles blow! We jump over our ledge. Run forward, up the hill. Running with four legs, stopping on two to shoot, back to running! Male trooper beside me hit. Falls down. I keep running.

We watch the rebels' trench as we run. Some shooting, but then they are running away! Only a few stay, all the others are running. We start the howling. First on our right, then down the line to left and back again. More rebels jump up and run. Some of the third try to howl with us. We are laughing. They can't howl, but they try. Then they start to cheer. Running up the hill. We howl, the third cheers, the rebels run.

I jump over their ditch. One of them throws away his rifle. I knock him down and keep running. We know that our hard trucks are behind them. We just keep pushing them on until they run into the trucks. They are all surrendering. A trooper ahead of me is coming back with a rifle over his back and another in his teeth. The officers say stop. The howling begins again. The third and the thirty-first take the red hill.

The Featureless Plain

This was the story I told to my old friend, Sebastian, sitting at the small tables, under the awning, while the people went about their affairs in the sunlit street.

When I was young, I felt a different wind. It blew on this side of my face, you see? Here, where I brush my hair back with my left hand. That's where it blew, if you follow me.

We were all young together, at the same point in our lives. We sat together and drank, some talked more intensely than others, some brooded with intense silence that said, at least to me, there is a man who wants to seem deep. None of us had anything real over which to brood, but some were attracted to that sad affect.

I was not. I played at studying, tried to be serious about science and engineering and mathematics. But there was always some pointless question on an exam, beginning with the phrase "... on a featureless plane, ignoring friction and gravity ...", and I could never get beyond that notion, For one thing, I always read plane but thought plain, and that always led me off into a dream, standing on a featureless plain, covered with sweet grass and small, blue flowers. I would form vague ideas about how I would populate that imaginary country. Women's voices singing old songs, cranes calling as they flew overhead ... I was not made to be a technician.

And then the wind shifted. The people around me, especially the people with authority and control, began to look this way, you see? I look at you over my right shoulder. I see you understand. I had bills to pay, rent to pay, I had to feed myself. And so I became ... what I became. But I was never good at it, and though I rose from post to post, it always came grudgingly, both on their part and on my own. You understand who I mean by "they".

And so when the rules, and the need to follow them, and especially the war required that I be given a genuine position of authority, it turned out to be here, here on a plain that is in fact almost featureless. The enemy are not too far off, but there aren't too many of them, no more than there are of us, really. And all we have to do is keep things from becoming so unfortunate that the people higher up - again, I glance to my right, you see? - will feel they have to lend a hand.

Why am I being obtuse? It's a long practiced habit. But you and I have a common point of view, I think. So I will be clear. I have had to pretend to be a good fascist, but like you, I believe, I never gave up my youth, and when we began to fight the socialists, I avoided the military and the law, and I tried to steer my life into offices and positions where I could quietly behave as something else while looking like a man of the party. But then I was posted here, here where it was thought I would at least do no substantial harm, here where I am in charge. And here where that miserable bastard Ramón was.

You knew him, of course. Clawed his way up in the army. Wore the uniform with apparent pride. Never a hair out of place. Became finally a full lieutenant, commanding a whole company of a conscript regiment. And had it all his own way here until I replaced the old official. The man who let Ramón have his way. Suddenly I was in his way.

I watched him closely. I knew better than he what assets the government had, capabilities for finding out about people. There are ways to know what a man is and what he used to be. I had better access to those ways than Ramón would, once he found about them, but even so, he would be able to find things about me. And I could never find anything about him that would be discreditable in the eyes of certain people. Again, I look down at my right hand. You see?

Meanwhile, I was also finding out about the people here and the land and the things that were needed to make it something of a better place. I could see that just a small amount of money in the right places might turn into more food for the men and women and children living in these little features scattered around the plain. Left to myself, I could make things slightly better than I found them. But everywhere I looked, I found that Ramón would find out.

I knew of another man, a man nearly ready to be promoted, and I knew how I might contrive to have him posted here, if only Ramón were ... not. Someone with whom I would be better matched. You follow me? But how to accomplish that adjustment? If I made an enemy of Ramón, I would regret it. As I suggested, there are things to be learned about what I have been, and what I did once, and possibly worst, things I never got around to doing. So he must go, I reasoned.

I could not reenact Solomon and Uriah the Hittite. There was no reasonable pretext for sending him and his company into war. Even if I had orders to fight, there was no enemy formidable enough to be sure Ramón would die or be injured or fail. He might even win a small skirmish, and then he would be more dangerous than before.

But then I thought, define what you fear and make it serve you. I don't remember where I read that, but it has a great amount of sense contained in a small phrase. I asked myself what I feared, and it was simple. I was afraid Ramón would get rid of me by denouncing me as a backslider or a sympathizer. What then if I denounced him? I dismissed the thought at first. There was nothing to suggest that he was anything but what he was, in the record. Ah, in the record. But a skillful traitor would keep his record clean, would he not? The absence of evidence is not, of course, evidence of absence.

But Ramón was not a traitor, at least in the legal sense. He was a single-minded buffoon, but that's the definition of a good fascist. How would he react to an accusation? He would become infuriated. He would curse socialists. He would say many things. And if he said those things in the hearing of ... ah.

In the early morning hours, I had Ramón arrested. He struggled, he argued, he was very angry. I told him his crime was known and that he deserved to be shot. I told him that I had nothing against him as a man, but that my duty was clear. Clear, that is, with a small exception. If he so loved socialism that he worked his way into our army and pretended to be a true fascist warrior in order to further socialism's cause, then I honored at least his dedication. And so I would let him desert.

This infuriated him. He raved for five minutes at me and at the soldiers I had brought with me. I said I admired his passion and his skill as an actor, but that my mind was clear. We took him in a vehicle quietly out into the plain, and everyone left behind assumed he was going to be shot. After we were out of sight of the camp, we turned east. We put out large white flags, turned on the lights, and drove slowly. I had never driven over this ground, and I found it remarkable how smooth and unremarkable it felt. I wondered if the wheels were crushing things or even leaving marks, but it was dark and there was no way to tell. With only a small half-globe of light around us, the plain seemed truly featureless.

I see the light is beginning to dawn for you. You anticipate me. But let me finish my story. This is the only time I have told it, and you are the only one I would trust to understand.

After a few kilometers, we stopped. We could see the enemy coming out with lights to examine us. They stopped a few meters away, and I walked out part way toward them. One of their officers came out to meet me. I was dressed very correctly, wearing my suit and my two civilian medals. He had a green uniform and a red star on his cap. We greeted each other, and I said that I had come to arrange a prisoner exchange. He asked how many prisoners I had. I said one. He said that, alas, he had none to exchange. I said that was not a difficulty. I pointed out that I was not a military man, and I was less concerned with exact procedures and protocols than an officer might have been. I said I merely wanted to return to him one of his own people, an incompetent spy, a man I hesitated to shoot, so little real harm had he done.

I had to explain it once more, but he finally understood me and agreed to accept Ramón, the failed spy. I said he was bound and gagged because he was very drunk when we arrested him, and I was afraid he would injure himself. I said we would just place him on the ground, turn our vehicle around, and leave. The officer agreed. As I turned, he asked me, hesitantly, if this was not a very unusual way of doing things?

I said yes, speaking in his language. But I asked him if the alternative would not be even more unusual? Did he think that I myself was a secret socialist, turning over to him, also a socialist, a fascist bastard? A man I sincerely hoped he would shoot? He agreed with me that it was most unlikely, and we drove away.

Waren Trust *2017*

In my small city, there's a stretch of land along the river. The downtown area surrounds it, but it's open and treated as an unnamed park. Someone told me that it belongs to the city, but the tables and benches in it are put there by businesses, and the gravel walk from one end to the other is likewise maintained by the merchants. It's not a long way from my apartment, and I go there on summer evenings to sit and write.

This week, I walked along the main street toward the open space, and there were two women walking ahead of me. The younger one was someone I'd seen before, a person with short, dark hair and black eyebrows. The older woman was new to me. She was speaking earnestly to the other one and sometimes making gestures with her hands. As we came to the entrance to the river land, they were joined by Airey, a man who was always wandering around in the downtown area, aimless and harmless, and usually with nothing to say. He simply dropped into step with them, walking along behind and eating from a bag of popcorn, one kernel at a time.

I took my usual place, on the town side, where there was a chair and a small table. I didn't want to be joined by anyone, so I left the long picnic-style benches to others. The two women sat down at a bench, facing each other. Airey sat down on the grass a few feet away.

In a few minutes, more people came in, either taking up seating or laying down towels or beach blankets to sit on. This was new, not something I'd seen before. If they said anything at all, it was too low to overhear, and the couple who sat down on the grass near me said nothing.

Then two men stood up and walked to the middle of the path. They stood back to back. Both were wearing khaki pants and white dress shirts, no ties, no jacket. Together, they raised both their arms and said "Waren Trust" in voices that carried. Everyone stopped talking except the older of the two women who came in with me.

I couldn't make out what her words were, but it was clear she was trying to persuade or influence the other person. The younger woman with the eyebrows said nothing for a moment, and then quite clearly said "Waren Trust". She made a finger-to-the-lips sign. The other woman raised her voice, saying "But Celia, please ..." Celia shook her head. The other woman got up, turned, and nearly tripped over Airey, then walked away, back up toward the street. Airey picked up the popcorn kernel she'd made him drop, ate it, and sat still. The two men on the path raised their hands again and said "Waren Trust."

As I watched, the men began to walk up and down among the other people, saying things that for the most part I couldn't hear. One came near enough that I heard him say "crisis of confidence". It seemed to be Celia he was speaking to. This went on for almost fifteen minutes.

Then two men came down from the street at the other end of the area. I stared at them, because they were both dressed in grey Edwardian suits and both had top hats. One carried a walking stick. The two leaders, if that's what they were, of the group saw them and moved to place themselves in their path. The newcomers paid no attention, and as they got closer, I could hear that they were talking about the open area itself.

"Yes," one of them said, "it is strange that it's just here, left undeveloped."

"I know," said the other, "but apparently the merchants would rather have people here than more businesses."

" I suppose. But I did hear another story. About an asylum that was here." At this point, the group leaders stood in front of them, blocking the way. One of them said "Shhh. Waren trust."

The men in costume stepped around the leaders, and the one who'd been interrupted continued. "There's something about being able to hear the voices of the inmates, still speaking." They continued their stroll. As they passed me, I heard one say "Gibberish, it's supposed to be. Just nonsense phrases." They strolled on, up and onto the shopping street.

A drop of tree sap fell close to my notebook, and I got up. One of the leaders looked at me, but I ignored him and walked away. Airey got up and followed me out.

The next evening the sky was supposed to be clear. The sunset would make glowing red light on the water and, as the sun dropped lower, on the backs of the stores. I went down to the area again. This time, my usual table was occupied, but I sat at the end of one of the benches. Shortly, it began to fill up with the same group that had been there the night before.

The difference was that the leaders had brought another man with them. He was a very large person, dressed in jeans and a horizontally-striped T-shirt, like a matelot. He wore a dark sport coat over it. When the leaders began their "Waren Trust" announcements, he said nothing. He just stood between them on the path, looking around.

Just as the leaders began their circulation among the group, the Edwardians returned. Their conversation grew louder as they approached, and the one with the cane was swinging it at the heads of dandelions as he walked. The topic was investments, something to do with exchange-traded funds and a shift of investor confidence toward corporate and away from municipal bonds. They ignored everything but each other, even when they came up against mister striped shirt. He held his arms wide, blocking their way. They sidestepped him and came together again on the path.

The big man then moved up behind them and took each one's collar in one of his hands. He lifted them up to tiptoes and gave them a quiet, professional bum's rush down the path and out of the area.

One of the leaders came by the bench where I was sitting, said something meaningless to one of the people, and then stopped across the table from me. I turned my notebook to a page where I'd written a rude phrase in large letters, showed it to him, and made my departure.

I wasn't pleased with the way things had gone, and I considered staying away, but by 5:30 the next afternoon, my curiosity took over. I bought a sandwich to bring along and went back to the place. This time I was early enough to get my chair and small table, and I quickly took possession. The group gathered as it had before, and the leaders brought their large colleague with them again. For almost half an hour, nothing unusual happened. Then the costumed pair returned. This time, as they strolled side by side, discussing some regulatory topic, they were followed by two municipal police officers.

As the little parade reached the center of the path, the big man stepped in front again. The leaders walked up behind him. The Edwardians halted, still talking, and the police came around from behind. One of them placed his hand on the striped chest and pointed toward the exit behind him. One leader came forward, but got the same treatment from the other officer. The two gentlemen paid no attention. They just kept talking about property tax abatements. Everyone else sat very quietly, watching the proceedings.

The big man and one of the leaders turned around and began walking away. The other leader said something to the police and tried to push the officer's hand away. In a series of dance steps, he was spun around, handcuffed, and almost carried off, back the way the police had come. To my disappointment, he didn't complain as he was taken away, not even to say "Waren Trust."

Since that night, the group hasn't shown up, nor have the Edwardians. The only thing of interest is Airey, eating popcorn and watching the ducks on the river.

For easily the fortieth time, Tennant was flipping through a tattered reprint of Gerard Manly Hopkins. On the table beside it was a transcription of Hopkins' letter in which he explained his sprung rhythm and his unorthodox sonnet structure. For Tennant, reading the poems aloud to himself had never explained the idea clearly, and so he was trying something new, re-reading the technique description, then turning to a poem itself, looking for evidence that the technique was really there. He had and so far kept a suspicion that Hopkins wrote what came easily and clearly to mind, retrofitting the theory to the work. He was so absorbed that he missed a tentative knock on the frame of his open door.

"Excuse me, please, Señor Jim?" said the man outside, speaking in Spanish.

Tennant was neither surprised nor annoyed. Two or three times a day, the same man came upstairs to him, asking for help or guidance or a translation of something minor. He was the owner and main employee of a small café, and Tennant was his tenant in one of the two rooms above it.

"Yes, Felix," he said, turning partly around.

"Señor Jim," the man said, still speaking in the language that Spanish had become, here in this small place, "There is a woman here. She cannot speak so that I understand it."

"She doesn't speak Spanish? What language is it?"

"It is the English."

"Ah. Well, I'd better come down."

It was not particularly an event for someone to turn up and be unable to communicate, even on this uninviting coast. When the cruise ships went by, they went far out to sea, avoiding the coral reefs and the unsheltered beach. Occasionally, a yacht would drop anchor and send someone ashore to buy drinks or provisions or to ask for some kind of assistance. None of those things was available, typically, although Tennant could at least offer advice and directions. Now, he put his jacket on over his slightly worn shirt and went down the stairs.

The café had four tables inside and a few more out along the street. It was unusual for more than one to be occupied. This morning, no one was there at all except a young woman sitting alongside a pair of large bags, clearly luggage. She was doing something with a phone, but she looked up when Tennant came in. Their host vanished back into the kitchen.

"Good morning," Tennant said. "I'm James Tennant. Can I help in some way?"

She looked at him with an expression of doubt, touched with a little concern. "Well, I hope so. Are you ... in charge here? I'm here by accident, and I need to get to Saint Angelo."

"To Saint Angelo? But ... this is Corazón. The island of Corazón. Saint Angelo is forty miles north."

"Right. I'm on the wrong island. The ferry boat didn't say it was landing here first. I thought it was the end of the line. I got off and tried to find somebody for directions. And then the boat left."

"And they told you to come and see me, I'm guessing."

"Well, they said I should come over here, anyway. Doesn't anyone speak English here?"

"No, not many people, I'm afraid."

"Well, anyway, how can I get the boat to come back and get me? I need to get to Saint Angelo. For a meeting."

She was dressed in a mixture of casual and modern professional styles. Her shoes, for example, were practical and athletic, right for travelling. She was wearing a jacket that looked hot for this climate, though. The shirt under it wouldn't have stopped a mosquito bite, let alone the sun's rays. He put her at late thirties.

She looked closely at him and saw a tall man, well past middle age and showing signs of it. His clothes were almost a camouflage, making him look like the rest of the population. The exception was that he had on a tan jacket, bleached almost to white, matching the loose, shapeless trousers of everyone else. Also, he wore shoes. They were dusty, made of tan leather with canvas panels at the sides.

He gestured at her phone. "Is that a satellite phone? I'm afraid that just a cellular one isn't going to be very useful."

"Why?"

"Well, are you getting any signal? 'Bars', that is?"

"No, nothing. I tried to get my office or the people I'm meeting, but it's not working."

"Yes, well, that's really what people experience here. There's just no coverage."

"Maybe if I charged it? Is there an outlet somewhere?" She glanced around the room.

"Ah, well, no. You only get power here someplace where there's a generator. And I'd be surprised if that helped, anyway. If you need to call someone, we can go to my office."

"All right. What kind of ... I mean, are you an official?"

Always that question. Always the dissatisfying answers. "I was, yes. I was with the Department of ..." He mentioned a large, gray, national organization. "I've retired."

"Oh," she said. "I don't think ... no, I don't know anybody there. In Washington, I mean. Is it a long way?"

"A long way?"

"To your office."

"Oh, no. Nothing's very far, here. Just down the street."

"Can I leave my bags? Or can we get somebody to carry them?"

Tennant sighed, mentally. For a dollar, any one of three people in the building would carry her bags. And if she left them sitting where they were, no one would lay a finger on them. But, just for situations like this, there was a closet in the owner's rooms with a large, ostentatious lock. "I ... we could have them brought along. But easier just to secure them here."

"Oh, great. Um, I should introduce myself, though. I'm Maryanne Fielding. I work for ..." She named a vast, global airline. "It's a sales meeting. In Saint Angelo."

"I almost never fly," he said. "Here, everything is by boats. Excuse me just a moment." He stepped back into the kitchen. Felix had, of course, been listening, uselessly since the conversation was in English, but listening anyway. The pattern was always the same. Señor Jim would speak with the confused person, they would go to his office to use the radio, and one of

71

the sons of the house would lock up the bags. All he needed was the cue, and all Tennant had to do was confirm it.

"Felix, this lady and I will go to the office so she can contact her people. Will you please have one of your young men bring her bags upstairs?"

"Of course, Señor. Is she badly lost?"

"She got off the ferry at the dock, thinking it was Saint Angelo. Benito or someone over there sent her to you and me."

"Will she need to stay, at all?"

"Please get a room ready for her. Unless her people can send a plane, she'll be here at least until tomorrow."

"There is no plane on Saint Angelo, Señor. Not today. It flew over this morning, going to Mata Gordo, as it always does on a Thursday."

"Well, then get a room ready, for certain. I will explain it to her."

"Yes, Señor."

He walked back out into the front room. "We can go now, if you're ready," he said. "A young man will lock up your bags."

"Oh, great."

In the full sunlight, the village – the only village – on Corazón was almost unremittingly white. There hadn't been any serious commerce for decades, and while there were a few businesses, there was little in the way of scavenged wood, reused panels, obsolete bill boards with garish colors. What there was in Corazón was brick, used and used again, over and over, and painted white outside, plastered inside. The sun glared off it in irregular triangles where the palm trees left gaps. People walked in slow zigzags from one patch of shade to another. There was no traffic except by foot. In the whole village, there were three functioning cars and a Jeep.

"So," Fielding said, "you've got the only working phone?"

"Well, no, not exactly. Over on the other side of the island, where you landed? They have a real radio. You know, with a microphone and an antenna. They need it to talk to the ferry and so on. But there's no one with enough English to help you with it. What I have is a satellite phone, and that *is* the only one."

"That's amazing. How do people ... Wait. What country is this?"

"Well, it's a US territory. It's the United States, technically. But we're not a state."

"Okay. That's good. I was afraid for a minute there ..."

"No, no. It wouldn't be impossible, down here, to wander into another country. But unless you did it in someone's small boat, somewhere along the line you'd have had to show a passport."

"Good." They'd walked about the equivalent of a block, and Tennant stopped at a gate, standing by itself. The fence it used to belong to had vanished, but there was a beaten walk behind it, leading to a door in another white brick building. There was no sign, and drapes were pulled across the one facing window. "Here we are."

Inside, it was dark and slightly cooler than the outside temperature. In the murky light, she could see a kind of front room, with a desk. There was no one sitting at it. There were also three wooden chairs, two of them in front of the desk and one immediately beside it. A light rectangle on the painted wall suggested a picture or a sign, something that had been there a long time and was then taken down.

"Wait here just a minute," Tennant said. "I'll have to go and start the generator." He vanished through a door behind the desk. She heard another door open, somewhere further back in the building, and then a series of mechanical sounds, repeated at short intervals. She recognized them as a gas engine's recoil starter cord being pulled. After six or seven repetitions, the engine started, stumbled once, and then settled down to run. Above her head, a light came on. Tennant came back into the front room.

"Why ..." she started. "Why do you need a generator for the phone?"

"It uses up batteries very quickly. Since I never know when I'll need it, I just leave it over here, sitting in its charger, and run it from the generator when I have to. God knows how much a new battery would cost."

It took another ten minutes to power on the phone and get a response from someone. Tennant left her alone while she explained her problem. The person she was talking to seemed unsurprised by the situation. He took down phone numbers and names and then, while she waited, called her office and the people at the conference she was missing. Finally, she came back out into the sunlight and found Tennant waiting for her.

73

"I'm finished," she told him. "They got the boat to come for me tomorrow. Somewhere around ten, they said."

"Oh, good. Hold on here a minute, and I'll go shut things down." After a pause, she heard the generator stop. He came outside shortly after and locked the door.

"There was a lizard in there," she said. "A little one."

"Very small? An inch long or so?"

"Yes."

"Those are young anoles. They eat insects. They're harmless to us. There are iguanas here as well, but they're much larger." He held his hands apart to demonstrate. "Harmless, too, though."

"I wasn't worried about it. I just don't tend to see ... wildlife ... all that much, while I'm on the phone."

"One of our many advantages," he said. They started walking back the way they'd come.

"So, that's that?" she asked. "Anything more we need to do?"

"No, nothing. Felix has a room for you, and his place is really the only place to eat. You could walk along the beach here if you like. No one will bother you."

"Actually, I'm suddenly tired. Could I just go back and lie down for a while?"

"Of course. And I'll let Felix know when to have dinner for you. For us, actually. It's not all that common for anyone else to eat there, and I'll have to help with the menu. It's a verbal one, I'm afraid. Really a case of whatever he has, prepared in one or two ways." He stopped. "You don't have a problem with seafood, do you?"

"No. Fish is fine. I'm not crazy about squid."

"It's not likely there'll be any squid. Felix doesn't like them much, himself. Someone will have caught a snapper, though, probably. It'll be somewhat plain, but fresh. Very fresh."

"All right. So, I'll rest for a while, and then ... when?"

"Oh, six or seven. Call it seven?"

"Fine." They'd reached the café. "I'll go speak to Felix. Just go up the stairs and turn right. Yours is the first door, and it won't be locked."

At first, she didn't sleep, but it was a relief to lie back and close her eyes. After a while, she got out some of the material for the meeting and tried to read it over again. That did put her into at least an uneasy doze and then something more like unconsciousness. She woke suddenly, and she realized that if she made these people hold up the meal for her, she'd be almost as embarrassed over that small failing as over getting off the boat on the wrong island.

When she came downstairs, there was no one in the tiny dining room, but there were plates and utensils for two, set out on the most sturdy-looking of the few tables. Tennant came out of the kitchen. After pleasantries lasting just a minute or so, Felix brought out a large plate with a pinkish roasted fish and some quartered potatoes. Tennant went back with him and returned with a bottle of wine and another one of water.

They ate slowly. She wasn't expert in picking a fish apart, even after Felix had divided it between their plates. It was astonishingly good, though, and she said so.

"That's one of the good things you get here. It was caught today, and there's nothing much wrong with the water it came from. It's too shallow for boats to get in close and dump anything."

He was wearing the same off-white jacket and slacks, and his shirt was open at the collar. His complexion was light for the climate, but she remembered him putting on a broad-brimmed hat when they went out to make the phone call. His face showed some of the lines of age, but the skin was tight and most of wrinkles were around the eyes.

"So, I think you told me," she said, "but it didn't stick. How long have you lived here?"

"I came here in 2004."

"And ... well, we *are* in the US, right? I think that's what you said."

"Nationally, yes. We're not part of any state. It's a territory. Like the Virgin Islands."

"But you weren't born here, though?"

"No. I was in the State Department, but there were changes there. Some reductions in budget. And so I took a position with the Department of the Interior. And came down here."

"And then you retired? And they didn't send anyone else?"

"No. There are only three hundred people, give or take, living here. And there aren't any ... problems that an official could deal with, anyway. So anything that needs an official hand or eye gets handled by my old superiors in Saint Thomas. Now I'm ... well, *an old man, driven by the Trades to a sleepy corner.*"

"What?"

"Sorry. T. S. Eliot. A piece called *Gerontion.*"

She thought about that. It was getting darker, and Felix came out from the kitchen with an oil lantern. "What do you mean, there aren't any problems?" she asked.

"Well, people aren't dying in the streets. The only natural threats are hurricanes, and any building still standing was shored up against bad weather decades ago. Nobody's invading, and no one here wants to invade anywhere else."

"But ... illegal immigration?"

"To where? Or from where? The people who want to leave, leave. Anyone who's still here wants to be. And no one from elsewhere could come here. There's no available land. It's all owned by someone."

"There's no power, though. No water. No ... " She paused. "What about doctors?"

"Well, there is water. There are wells, up in the center of the island. And people have tanks that they fill from there. Power ... well, people get along with batteries or they just don't. Healthcare, yes, that's a gap. If you have a heart attack here, you have to be evacuated to one of the larger islands."

"So those aren't problems?"

"You and I, sitting here over dinner, think they are. But could you write a check to put a clinic here? Or set up wind power generators? I can't. And the Department made a conscious decision not to."

"But don't the people care? Don't they complain?"

"The children take the ferry – that one you were on – over to the bigger island. For school. Every year, a handful of them don't come back. The ones who do either stay for a while and leave, or they settle here. So far, there's always been a core who stay. Usually the oldest son or daughter. They inherit the little plots of land, and they keep working them. I don't think the population's changed by more than one or two percent, the whole time I've been here."

"Amazing. So, we – I mean, the US – we don't ... " She made a looking-for-the-words movement with her hands. "Don't we have a responsibility ...?"

"Interesting. You're going through all the questions I had, except I had them before I got here. Before I knew Corazón existed. "

"Really? And ... answers?"

"I did come up with a few. They have to do with scale, mostly. And history." He looked out through the open door. "It won't be full dark for another hour, give or take. Would you like to hear the history part, at least?"

"Sure."

"This is a small, boring island. It doesn't have a lot of history, and only one even vaguely dramatic episode. No one has any idea what went on here, prior to about 1570. The Spanish sailed around it a few times and finally landed. There's a hint that there were people here before, but no real evidence. They would have been Taino people from South America, just as there were on other islands down here. If they were here, they vanished very shortly after European contact, and there's no record of how or why. European diseases would be a good guess.

"And then, the place was essentially left empty. It's not good for sugar cane for some reason. I'm not really an expert in botany or agriculture, but it just isn't. So the Spanish came and went, periodically, landing in emergencies, maybe raising pigs for portable food. The people who stayed were mostly mixed European and African, refugees or escapees or slaves. And again, because it wasn't good for anything commercially useful, and it was so small, it wasn't worth much attention. That went on for four hundred years, more or less."

"Four hundred years?"

"Yes. And all that time, it was technically a Spanish colony, but not even a remotely interesting one."

"But now it's ours?"

"Well, accidentally. We fought our only real imperial war right at the end of the 1800s because we could. Everybody else was doing it, France and England especially. So we took the Philippines and Cuba away from Spain, and that deal brought in a few of these little islands, too. And so, there we were."

"The US fought a war with Spain?"

"Yes. In 1898. There was an irresponsible press then, too. Just newspapers, of course, but it was very effective in whipping up support for a war. And we won. Not without some embarrassing mistakes, but we did win. And then we had to deal with the outcomes. And Corazón was one of them."

She had a sudden memory from her undergraduate experience; she'd had an economics professor who lectured in the same way Tennant was talking. He used incomplete sentences and strung them together with "and" in the same pattern. Her impression at the time was of a man speaking from notes and trying to make it sound as though it was off the cuff.

"So they didn't do anything for the island at all?"

"The government didn't want any more little unprofitable islands than they already had. The Philippines went into full blown revolution against us, almost as soon as the Spanish were out. And there were favors to repay, too. So they gave a perpetual lease on this place to a friend of a politician, basically leaving it up to him. That lasted until 1916, and then they prosecuted him and took the island back."

"Prosecuted him? For what?"

"It should have been for rape, homicide, slavery, and fraud, but it was easier to just indict him for tax evasion. There's one master's' thesis from 1932 that talks about it. Otherwise, it's forgotten."

"No legal records?"

"Lost in a fire, apparently. But the point is, the population of the whole island was just a hundred or so people by then. And there was clear evidence that it was no place to try to make a profit. The lessee may have been a bandit, but he tried everything he could think of to squeeze a dollar out. He was very thorough."

"So the US just walked away? Just left the island on its own?"

"Well, not completely. They kept a presence here ... people like me ... for quite a while. Then I retired, and they took the opportunity to save a few dollars. And they let me keep the keys to the old office."

"That seems kind of cheap. Kind of ... what's the word?"

"Callous? But no, not really. There's only a handful of people here. And they own what they own. They grow enough and catch enough to live on. And those who want to leave can leave. They're citizens. If they move to an actual state, they can vote."

"But still ..."

"No, I really think it's for the best. Leaving well enough alone, essentially."

Fielding looked skeptical. She glanced around the small room. He saw where she was looking.

"And I know," he said, "You're looking at Felix's little establishment and thinking that it's the only commercial enterprise on the island. But the fishermen and the people who grow food sell some of what they have. It's not wholly subsistence. Given the scale, it's actually remarkable that there's a café and ... a place with rooms at all."

"But who stays here? Who eats here?"

"I do. And the occasional accidental guest." He looked at her. "Maybe I'm biased. I grew up with some references and some ideas, and then I had some experiences. And then I came down here and really didn't have the chance to gather any more outside perspective. But there are a few things I think of often. Films, for instance. I haven't seen them for years, but they stay with me."

The bottle of wine stood between them. It was a white of some kind, from Virginia. Fielding had sipped on hers without much enthusiasm, and there was still some in the glass. Tennant had finished his, and she'd automatically poured him more, just because the bottle was closer to her.

"Films?" she asked.

"Gillo Pontecorvo's 'Burn', for example. An English rogue fomenting and betraying a revolt on a colonial island. Or 'Cobra Verde' by Herzog. A revolutionary sells out. My reading of them was *let it alone. First, do no harm. Don't meddle with things you don't understand.* 'Battle of Algiers' is another."

"I haven't seen those."

"No, they're almost antiques." He took a long drink from his water glass, then sipped on the wine. "Arthur Clarke wrote a short story called 'The Next Tenants'. A man is on one of the islands near the ones used for the post-war atomic tests. He's training termites to take over when humanity destroys itself, giving them the wheel and eventually fire. I'm sure Clarke didn't mean it that way, but I always thought of it as another *leave it alone* narrative." He sipped at the wine again.

"So you're leaving things alone here?"

"Not entirely. I do help a bit. Sometimes." There was a pause. "Another work I like to think about is a book written as a memoir. Talking about the last few years of our time in Vietnam. There was a man in it and a woman, sort of bureaucrats. They were both disillusioned, but the man kept on with it all. The woman quit, left, went back to the US. The man went out on one of the last helicopters. But he never saw her again."

"What was the book?"

"It never had a title. It wasn't published."

She saw that a glass and a half of wine had produced an effect. Tennant's speech was still precise, accentless American English, but there was a change in tone, and he blinked more often. Suddenly, two thoughts came together for her. "*You* wrote it, am I right?"

"No," he said, looking out past her shoulder. "I didn't. I never did write it."

She watched his face. He wasn't staring off into infinity or looking down at the floor. His eyes moved in time with his breathing, looking at a faded poster Felix had tacked to the wall, glancing at a lateral crack in the interior plaster, the bottle of wine. "I'm sorry," she said. "I didn't mean ..."

"No, not at all. Of course not. Don't mention it." He was still looking at other things, not at her.

"If you did write it, just write it down, even. Not publish it, necessarily ..."

"No, really. I never ..."

"You might feel better."

At that point, he did look at her. "I don't feel bad. It's not any kind of major ... issue. For me." He looked away again.

"Mm." It was almost inaudible, a small noise she made when someone had lied, and the situation made it injudicious either to disagree or agree. It wasn't an *I'm thinking* noise or a placeholder or even any sort of reply. All it meant was that she'd heard something, and there was no need for the speaker to repeat it.

Tennant stood up, making a clumsy set of movements in the process, pushing the chair back, steadying himself with a hand on the table top. "I'll let Felix know we're done. We should be on our way over to the docks by at least nine tomorrow."

"Fine."

"Do you have what you need ... that is, do you need anything in your room?"

"No. I think I'm all set."

"Very well, then. I'll see you in the morning." He picked up the bottle and a glass and took them back into the kitchen.

In the morning, she came down with her bags, retrieved by a silent young man from the symbolic closet. Tennant was already there, finishing a cup of coffee. He said, "good morning" in a precise, formal way. She returned it. They dealt briefly with the issue of paying Felix. Credit cards were useless, but Tennant said he'd deal with it and send her a note. He assured her that it wouldn't be expensive.

"Would you like coffee? Breakfast is really just bread or toast, I'm afraid." She declined, showing him a packaged energy bar. They loaded her belongings into the same dusty Jeep that had brought her over the island's central hills. The driver started to get out, but Tennant waved him back behind the wheel. He opened the passenger's front door for Fielding, then got in the back himself.

"Oh," she said. "You don't have to come along if you ... if you're busy."

"Not at all. And there won't be many English-speaking people at the docks anyway. I'll make sure you're on your way."

81

"That I don't get on the wrong boat, you mean?"

"No, no. And there won't be more than one, anyway. But if for some reason, it doesn't show up ... I can swear in Spanish fairly well."

They turned at the end of the street, leaving the village behind instantly. The road went up the first of three switchbacks, up and over the central hills. The tires made a crisp sound on the dry gravel. No one said anything. Tennant appeared to be looking at the tops of trees and, when there was a view of it, out at the ocean. As they reached the crest and started down the other side, he pointed north. "Look there," he said, "A frigate bird."

Fielding looked where he was pointing, and she saw a huge bird, gliding on its long wings in a slant down toward the water. She nodded. They went around another curve, and the dock appeared. He pointed again, this time at the water. "The boat's coming. They managed to get it right, or there's someone ..." He stopped.

"Another idiot," she said. "Someone else who doesn't know what she's doing."

"No, no. That's not what I meant."

"Right. Anyway ... thank you, Mr. Tennant. It's been interesting. Different. And let me know if you write that book."

Twenty minutes later, the boat backed away from the dock. When it was unquestionably out of earshot, Tennant said aloud, "No. Thank you, but no. I won't."

The Bodies

2017

A short play

Characters

SAM: 40s, British or American.

LAURA: Also Western, similar age.

(Interior, an apartment or small house, SE Asia,
1946. The kitchen. Asian street sounds off. Sam is
doing some kind of meal preparation at a table. Laura
comes in left with cloth or net shopping bags of
unpackaged, local-looking groceries.)

LAURA

I'm back.

SAM

You are. How was the market?

LAURA

Packed. People seem to have money again, suddenly.

SAM

They do. I heard an actual motor vehicle just now.

(L is setting bags down.)

SAM

Can I help?

LAURA

Get the rice. Just inside the stairs door.

(SAM goes off, left. LAURA kicks off shoes, steps
into indoor sandals. Vehicle horn off, bicycle bell
ringing. Sam returns with large bag.)

SAM

That'll hold us for a day or two.

LAURA

Yes.

SAM

See anybody?

LAURA

Well, yes. I saw Roger Wiltinck coming out of a shop.

SAM

Really?

LAURA

He was wearing a dress.

SAM (Not startled)

Oh.

LAURA

I thought I was mistaken, but he recognized me. He was going to say something, I think, but then he just walked away.

(Pause. S and L lock eyes.)

SAM

The war's over, but ... still there are things ...

LAURA

I know. Things you can't say. We can't say.

SAM

This ... it's not earthshaking. It's not, oh, D-Day, or anything like that.

LAURA

And you're still not supposed to say.

SAM

But it's not fair ... there's no reason you shouldn't know. Hell, you worked with him.

LAURA

You don't have to say.

SAM

No, but it's not fair to you. But you still can't ...

LAURA (interrupts)

Can't tell anyone. I wouldn't, anyway. It's his business.

SAM

That's the funny thing. Not his. He's not Roger. He's Claire.

LAURA

What?

SAM

Claire Dragoniere. Belgian, not Dutch.

LAURA

You're serious? Roger is a woman?

SAM

Yes.

LAURA

Why?

SAM

That's a bit metaphysical, don't you think?

LAURA

Don't be a wiseacre. Why was he ... why was she doing ... that?

SAM

You remember, two years ago? Todd and I were closeted off by ourselves, planning something? And it was very much under wraps?

LAURA

I do. Most of the office was out of it, as far as I could tell.

85

SAM

There was this person, Roger. The Japanese supposedly
had him, up near Lashio. A Dutch journalist, he was
supposed to be. But he wasn't.

LAURA

All right.

SAM

He was from Holland, yes, but he'd been in the Dutch
fascist party. They had one. So did we, after all.
But the Germans helped send him out here, to assist
the Japanese.

LAURA

With intelligence?

SAM

They were supposed to get locals to leak it to us
that Roger was up there, on the run from them, and if
we rescued him, he could help us. Then they'd have a
double here. Feed us manure, give them good
information.

LAURA

That's classic.

SAM

Trouble was, we had more and better locals than they
did, and we knew all about it. That was what Todd and
I were pondering. How to profit from it, what to do
with or about Roger. If anything.

LAURA

But ... (makes circular motion with her hand)

SAM

But then we got more information from up north. There
was a real person, hiding out in the countryside with
the locals. A young woman.

LAURA

Claire?

SAM

Yes. Her father was in exports. On the coast. He died or he disappeared, anyway. Early on. But Cliare was in the country with him, and she got away. One of his local people got her out, and they hid her.

LAURA

And you went up there and got her! Those two weeks when you were away!

SAM

Right. Because Todd had this idea ... we rescue somebody, some European, from up there, bring him or her ... didn't really matter, we thought ... back here, and the bad folks would think it was Roger. And then we'd feed them rubbish instead of vice versa.

LAURA

That's such a Todd-like idea! I was always glad he was on our side.

SAM

Indeed. But Claire was even better than that. She was the right age. She'd cut her hair short for being in the jungle. Had on some soldier's fatigues when we met her. And I ... not Todd ... had the idea that she could really be Roger.

LAURA

My God! And she agreed?

SAM

She wasn't very ... oh, expressive, I suppose ... but, yes, she agreed. And I got the idea that she was happy to be doing something. Fighting, you know.

LAURA

I don't know about the fighting part, but she was definitely good at play-acting. I sat two desks down from him .. her ... for what, twenty months? ... and never guessed. And here's a secret you don't know. Min ... you know, Min, from the office? ... had a crush on Roger!

SAM

Really? Wonderful. I mean, not for Min, but good
reviews for Claire.

LAURA

But why the ... act? The masquerade?

SAM

There had to be someone visible working with us.
There were people of theirs here, keeping an eye on
us, just as we did up there with them. There had to
be a believable Roger, sitting in the office, doing
things.

LAURA

And so now? What's she going to do?

SAM

She's out. Going back to Brussels. Her mother's
there.

LAURA

What will the mother say, I wonder?

SAM

Well, she won't hear about the Roger part. That's
very undercover, still. The Mum was only told last
week that her daughter's alive and coming home. She
hadn't heard a thing.

LAURA

So Claire just goes home? What would she say to
someone, a husband or even children? "What did you do
in the war, Mummy?"

SAM

Hmm. I have no real way of knowing, of course, but I
got the impression that a husband wasn't really her
... goal in life. Just a guess. But she does have
quite a resume, now, for certain kinds of employment.

LAURA

Oh. I see.

SAM

Belgium's had a kind of shadow intelligence
organization through the war. Now they'll have to
build it into something real. And for damn sure
they'll need one.

LAURA

Oh, yes. Africa.

SAM

That stinking heap they've made in the Congo, for
example.

LAURA

Certainly. And you think that might be something
she'd be able to do?

SAM

No doubt in my mind. Todd gave her some names, he
said. People to talk with.

LAURA

It's amazing, still. I can't ... really get it
through my head. Oh ...

SAM

Yes?

LAURA

Did it work? Did it do any good?

SAM

Absolutely.

LAURA

Where?

SAM

That last-gasp push they tried, up along the Sittang.
Tried to break out?

LAURA

Right. It failed.

SAM

They sent one under-strength brigade into a gap in
our advance. The gap was actually quite full. One of
our divisions and one of the Chinese. They were shot
to bits before they even really started to advance.
Roger told them we'd left it unguarded.

LAURA

Score one for Roger.

SAM

Several hundred, in fact.

(L turns around, starts putting more groceries away.
S is doing something with the bag of rice.)

LAURA

One question occurs to me.

SAM

I can guess.

LAURA

What happened to the real Roger?

SAM (tonelessly)

He didn't survive the war.

LAURA

You killed him.

SAM

No. I didn't kill him.

LAURA

I see.

(L gets something from a cupboard. Gets down
something else. Her back is turned, and we can't see
what she's doing.)

SAM

The jungle is full of bodies. Up in the north,
something lying on the ground, long and covered with

moss and leaves and mud. It's more likely a bone than a stick. A year old or a hundred.

LAURA

They're all that way, I suppose. All the jungles, by now.

SAM

Right. Burma, the Congo, the Philippines. All the jungles.

(L turns with a highball glass in each hand, holding one out.)

LAURA

To the bodies.

SAM

The bodies.

(They drink.)

CURTAIN

The Station at Avignon

> *"I took Braque and Derain to the station at Avignon.*
> *I never found them again."*
>
> *- Picasso*

What a mess. She tried to keep everything held down to the pure tactical level. *Get the hell out of Chicago traffic.* Union Station was still a moderately clean and safe place. Outside, especially if you were driving a car, it was not. *Canal and Jackson. Get on 90, south to 94, screw the toll road, get out of here and back to Michigan.*

Joanna kept up the navigation narrative, speaking it aloud, leaving anything more analytical for the long drive back. Only the rail yards in Fuller Park reminded her of the train. Then she shut that off, making sure she stayed with I-94 as it made its giant bend to the east. Lake Michigan was still in the way, though, and the freeway turned south once more, past Deering until it finally made a sharp bend around the bottom of the lake and toward home. *Five hours at least, back to Ann Arbor.*

As the traffic eased off – *at least it's just going in one direction now* – she slowly relaxed her stomach muscles and took some long breaths. *Jack. And Stewart. Stewart and Jack. Not just leaving, have left.* She faced the necessity of deciding what she thought about that.

Both of the boys she'd brought down here – people in Michigan think of Chicago as *down* – were going away, joining the army together. Probably going to Vietnam. Jack, she'd met in class. Stewart was his high school best friend. Knowing Jack, apparently, meant knowing Stewart. Not in the biblical sense; she'd slept with Jack, but she and Stewart had never touched each other, not even to shake hands. Stewart was a painter, and he'd asked Jack if he thought Joanna might pose for him. Jack said, "Of course." Stewart never asked. Jack told Joanna, and she never brought it up, either.

Next week. Next week, I graduate. She was already working on applications, looking at master's programs. Her private self-image was a woman – slightly taller – in a lab jacket. Or in khaki shorts, crouching in a forest with a camera. She was aware of Jane Goodall and Marie Curie; she'd heard of Tatiana Proskouriakoff and Ursula Franklin. She knew, unusually for her time, the pitfalls a woman in science would encounter. *An undergraduate, fine. World's full of us. But try for grad school, watch out.*

She remembered her advisor's advice. "Getting in will be easier than getting on. The departments need graduate students – they're inexpensive, sometimes actually free labor. But they don't necessarily need more graduated degree holders. They can pick and choose."

Until this last year, the professors had been safely remote. Hard to grab somebody from up at the front of an auditorium. And the individual grads who taught face-to-face in undergraduate classrooms: mostly frantic, overwrought seekers. They'd all been young men, but withdrawn, frankly insecure young men. There was one postdoc who was whispered to be huggy, hippie, free-love-baby. She'd avoided his class sections. *I get enough of that at work.*

Waiting tables in a cheap red-sauce-Italian place. Women were only hired for the dining room. The attached bar and music space used young men, preferably big young men. But the management liked coeds, and the management worked both rooms. She shifted in the driver's seat, remembering the butt-pinch bruise. *Blue badge of courage. Never again.*

How to do that? She'd been on a prize scholarship, paying tuition and supplies, but room and board was on her. So she worked. Her parents helped a bit. But they'd already put the older brother through. *Mom and Dad. Moral support, but not much else.*

Jack. Jack, on his way to a war. She thought about his back story; guitar lessons from the age of 12, music school acceptance. His acoustic guitar wasn't the most highly-valued instrument, but he kept at it, picking up just enough piano to satisfy the department. He wrote a few pieces; she wasn't familiar with the classical canon of guitar, but his songs were pleasant to hear. Then one semester out from graduation, he'd just quit. And almost as if they'd been watching him, the draft board pounced.

And Stewart went, too. A recruiter lied, claiming he could guarantee they'd serve together. *Sheer bullshit.* They'd go where the dice roll sent them. At least they were going into boot camp together. When the day came, Joanna drove them to Chicago and the train. *Now, I'm driving back to school, by myself. Trying to decide how I feel about ... them. And things.*

Who did she know who'd tried to do grad school and a marriage? Or any kind of commitment, for that matter? A friend's older sister. One of the TAs in her department. Somebody said that one of the postdocs had a husband in Milwaukee. *Milwaukee. Jesus. How do you ... stay with somebody? Like that? That far away?*

And what if there were children? Honestly, how would that work? *Do I want children? Ever?*

Where would life go if she were connected to a musician? To Jack, for example? What would he have to look forward to? If he had a gig somewhere, *and I had ... a lab job, or something out in ... the woods?* Would he be any kind of father? Would he need mothering, himself?

Stewart. What if? *Oh, dammit! What if Jack ... is the one who doesn't come back?* Would Stewart ... want ... *me?* How does a painter even get paid? Does he get ... a teaching job? Like faculty or something? *And when he isn't painting ...* She remembered a few occasions when Stewart was between pictures. Sad. Far down. Not even Jack could cheer him up. *A Manchild in the Promised Land,* for sure. Mothering. He'd need it. *And so would a musician.*

She'd met a couple of Jack's friends. A drummer and his girlfriend. He and Jack sat out on the apartment's small patio. Joanna and the girlfriend stayed inside, drank part of a bottle of Gallo. *Hearty Burgundy.* Joanna learned some of the music way of life. Enough to make her wonder why anyone tried. *Gig to gig. Never any money. Always drinking somebody else's wine.*

I'm nobody's suburban mom. But ... How do you eat? How do you ever have a family? Or even a dog?

She swept her eyes across the dashboard. Her father taught her to check all the gauges once every five minutes. *You won't get surprised that way.* The gas was just touching the quarter-tank line. *Gas, yeah. Get a candy bar or something. Use the bathroom.* Shortly, there was an exit, and she pulled off. *Coloma. Never heard of it.*

In the restroom, she spent a few minutes staring at herself in the mirror. Her hair was long and very straight, coming out from under a starry headband and falling down below her shoulders. She had a pair of sunglasses in her canvas bag, and she put them on. *Move over, Michelle Philips. Or Grace Slick. Singing backup for somebody, maybe whacking myself on the ass with a tambourine.*

She shook her head, took the sunglasses off, and went back to the car. The station guy took twelve dollars from her, said "Got your windows nice and clean for ya, pretty lady."

"Good, thanks," she said. *You and the horse you rode in on.* She drove back out to the freeway. Mostly, driving didn't do much for her, but on entrance ramps she enjoyed the acceleration. Her car was a hand-me-down from her father, and he liked big V8 sedans. It moved when you stepped on the gas.

Merged back into the traffic, she forgot the gas station boy, and tried to focus on Jack, Stewart, and Vietnam. She didn't get very far, and her mind wandered. *What's on the radio, clear out here?* Her usual stations were out of reach. She let the radio seek a channel. The first offering was some kind of news. *No.* The next one was playing The Plastic Ono Band. *Working class hero.* She began parodying it, out loud. *A lurking class hero is something to be. How about shirking class? Smirking class?*

I'm never going to be working class. She didn't have the background. *Even at 21, I don't know how to do anything.* She wouldn't mind, necessarily, but almost anything manual took some knowledge. And body strength. But mostly, she didn't feel as though anything repetitive would be good. *I'm too curious. I want to try things.*

That's ... She stopped herself. *What was that? I just said something about myself. Damn.*

The song ended, and the radio began a summary of news. There was a semi in the way, and she was occupied with slipping out into the left lane. But she heard "... in other news, the photographer Diane Arbus has been found dead in her New York apartment, an apparent suicide."

Damn. I liked her. As soon as she said it, Joanna reflexively questioned it. *Why? She was ... independent. She didn't ... settle for things.* The radio went on to another story.

Joanna turned the noise off. Was Arbus a working class ... anything? *Some kind of hero. Yeah.* She sensed the onset of a brain worm. The Lennon song was repeating its refrain in her head. *Something to be ...* She remembered her own face in the bathroom mirror. *I should cut my hair.*

The Author

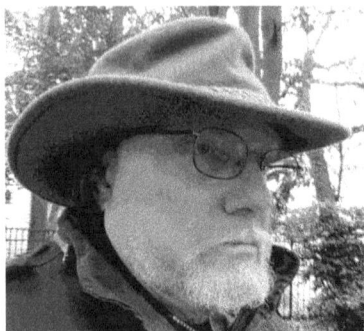

McConnell is in his sixties, retired from decades in technology. His parents were left-leaning intellectuals, living in a rural part of Michigan. His father was in the Art Department at Michigan State University.

The resulting exposure to the arts, social consciousness, horses, pickup trucks, farming, academia, dogs, and motorcycles gave McConnell what he admits is a mixed bag of world views and tastes.

Today, he writes a series of moral tales, thinly disguised as crime novels. In the intervals of writing long fiction, he also produces short stories, poems, song lyrics, and – so far one – short play. Many of them are included in this volume.

When he's not writing, he cooks; takes pictures of plants and animals; supports wildlife preservation and a kind of vindictive/progressive politics; and reads history and biography.

He lives in Ann Arbor with his wife and a dog.

He says: *"If you understand the ideas of normal distribution and of time as a series of points along a line, there isn't much in the universe that you can't at least imagine. You may not understand a thing, but you can beat it into one of those models. If you can do that, you can form an opinion that whatever it seems to be probably could exist or, no, it probably can't. Anything beyond that, you're on your own."*

Find the author's novels on Amazon Kindle
at *https://www.amazon.com/-/e/B00DQUQI16*

and additional material at the ProcArch blog.
http://procarch.blogspot.com/